*Law*Basics

DELICT

FOURTH EDITION

By

Gordon Cameron

Senior Lecturer in Law at the University of Dundee

W. GREEN  THOMSON REUTERS

12- 721680(4)

First published in 2002

Published in 2011 by W. Green, 21 Alva Street, Edinburgh EH2 4PS

Part of Thomson Reuters (Professional) UK Limited

(Registered in England & Wales, Company No 1679046.
Registered Office and address for service: Aldgate House,
33 Aldgate High Street, London EC3N 1DL)

www.wgreen.thomson.com

Printed and bound in the UK by CPI Antony Rowe,

Chippenham, Wiltshire

No natural forests were destroyed to make this product;
only farmed timber was used and replanted.

A CIP catalogue record for this title is available from the British Library

ISBN 978-0-414-01833-4

Thomson Reuters and the Thomson Reuters Logo

are trademarks of Thomson Reuters.

© 2011 Thomson Reuters (Professional) Limited

Crown copyright material is reproduced with the permission of the
Controller of HMSO and the Queen's Printer for Scotland.

In memoriam, Bill Stewart 1958–2010

Solicitor

Enthusiast for the law of delict

Source of great entertainment

Colleague

Friend

CONTENTS

TABLE OF CASES

ix

1. INTRODUCTION

THE PLACE OF DELICT IN SCOTS LAW

Delict and public law

Delict is an aspect of private as opposed to public law. This means that the law of delict regulates relations between private legal persons, whether individuals or corporations, as opposed to relations between the individual and the state. That said, civil remedies may be sought where state agencies have acted wrongfully and this brings delict into contact with administrative law which is a branch of public law. This is a developing area of the law given fresh impetus by human rights legislation.

Delict and criminal law

A clear distinction may be drawn between civil law, of which delict is part, and criminal law, which is another element of public law. Delict and criminal law both concern wrongdoing, but in different senses. Delict consists of a breach of a duty owed to another person or a wrongful act against another person. A crime is an offence against the criminal law. As delict necessarily involves some form of invasion of another person's rights and is not simply a transgression of the law, there can be no such thing as a victimless delict.

There are some areas of overlap, e.g. an assault may be the subject both of criminal proceedings and a civil action. An offence against the criminal law, however, is not necessarily a delict and a delict is not necessarily a crime. While in a criminal trial the prosecution must prove its case *beyond reasonable doubt*, in a civil case sufficient proof may be established on *the balance of probabilities*.

Where one person suffers loss as a consequence of wrongful behaviour and liability in delict is established, the wrongdoer or delinquent comes under an obligation to repair the harm. Thus the term reparation may be used instead of delict. Reparation, however, normally refers to monetary compensation in the form of damages and there are of course other remedies available in delict that may prove more suitable in the circumstances. In the modern law the aim of damages is to compensate the victim, not to penalise the wrongdoer. The criminal law imposes penalties and is mobilised by agents of the state who prosecute the accused in the criminal courts. The law of delict is mobilised by citizens or other legal individuals, and remedies, not penalties, are pursued in the civil courts.

Objectivity and the mental element

Liability in reparation under the common law requires *culpa*, that is fault, not *mens rea*. In criminal law mental fault (*mens rea*) is required in order to justify punishment. As the law of delict does not punish, this need for inquiry into the state of mind of the delinquent does not arise. Nevertheless, a rough comparison may be made. In the modern criminal law the tendency is to judge *mens rea* objectively by the standard of the reasonable person, rather than to look for corrupt and evil intention. In reparation the mental element concerns what the defender ought to have known or ought to have foreseen. Thus, as in the criminal law, the approach taken is objective.

When enquiring into harm caused unintentionally the question is whether a reasonable person in the position of the defender would have foreseen that their acts or omissions involved a risk of injury to the pursuer. Broadly, where there is a foreseeable risk there is a duty to take care, although this statement requires qualification as will become evident in the chapter on negligence. It is not a defence to establish that the defender did not in fact foresee a risk if they ought to have foreseen it, and what ought to have been foreseen is determined by reference to what the reasonable person would have foreseen.

When considering intentional harm it appears in most cases that the specific or direct intention to harm the pursuer need not be present since one is presumed to intend the natural and probable consequences of one's conduct. Intentional conduct may be culpable where an action is carried out deliberately in the knowledge that harm to the pursuer will be the likely result, irrespective of care taken. There appears to be no need to enquire into whether the defender did in fact know that harm would be the inevitable consequence; such knowledge can be imputed if it should have been evident to the reasonable person.

In the general case, just as in the criminal law, motive is irrelevant. However, there are exceptions in certain areas of delict. Liability for use of land, *in aemulationem vicini*, is dependent upon establishing malice. Malice is also the basis for liability in defamation, but, except where certain defences apply, malice is presumed and need not be proved. Motive is relevant in establishing conspiracy and in liability for inducing breach of contract.

Obligations

The Scotland Act 1998 s.126(4) divides Scots private law into the law of persons, the law of property, the law of obligations and the law of actions. This restates a Roman taxonomy. The same categories are found in Justinian's *Institutes* of A.D. 553. Delict is a branch of the law of obligations. An obligation is "a legal tie by which we may be necessitated or constrained to pay or perform something" (Stair, *Institutions of the Law of Scotland*, I, 3, 1).

The other branches of obligations are: contract; promise; unjustified enrichment; and *negotiorum gestio*. Contractual obligations and promise arise *ex voluntate*, that is by the will of the person taking on the obligation. People volunteer for such obligations. Obligations arising from unjustified enrichment and *negotiorum gestio*, on the other hand, arise *ex lege*—they are imposed by law in circumstances where justice requires that an action lie against the party enriched, but where there is no basis in agreement for a contractual obligation. Similarly, delictual obligations are imposed by law. Specifically, the obligation to pay reparation arises from wrongdoing; that is from the delict committed. While we are mostly concerned with reparation; that is the obligation to pay damages, there are other delictual obligations. For instance, a state of affairs amounting to nuisance will give rise to an obligation to abate the nuisance, enforceable by interdict. Delictual obligations, to make recompense or of restitution, will arise from wrongful use or possession of another's property. In certain limited circumstances, such as spuilzie, ejection and intrusion, there may arise an obligation to pay violent profits. Violent profits is a sum representing the maximum amount the pursuer could have made from the property had the defender not been in wrongful possession. In some delicts, e.g. breach of confidence, the defender can be compelled to disgorge any profits made out of the wrongdoing.

Delict and property law
There are areas of delict that are intimately related to property. Damage to or destruction of property may be the loss in respect of which damages are sought. Equally, delict may be invoked to protect property rights. As noted in the preceding section, wrongful use or possession of another's property gives rise to delictual liability. Intrusion is a delict committed by wrongful occupation of heritable property when the owner is not in possession and ejection is committed when the owner or rightful occupier of heritable property is wrongfully dispossessed. The right to exclusive use and possession of heritable property may be enforced under the laws of trespass, where the invasion is temporary, or encroachment, where it is permanent. The right to comfortable enjoyment of heritable property is protected by the law of nuisance. An operation conducted on land maliciously with the predominant spiteful purpose of harming a neighbour is actionable in delict *in aemulationem vicini*. Where excavations have deprived a neighbour's buildings of necessary support, actions have been raised in some cases in negligence, in others in nuisance. Moreover the occupation of heritable property incurs a statutory duty under the Occupiers' Liability (Scotland) Act 1960 to exercise reasonable care for the safety of persons entering on that property, breach of which incurs liability in reparation.

Delict has a clear position within the structure of Scots law. However, like all other elements, it is not a totally discrete body of law, it inter-relates with other areas of the law, in some instances, very closely.

RIGHTS AND WRONGS

The structure of delict
Stair is aptly described as the architect of modern Scots law. It is primarily Stair whom we have to thank for a systematic exposition of Scots law that allows it to be presented according to a coherent structure in which obligations occupy a clear location in relation to other aspects of private law, and contractual and delictual obligations are differentiated.

Stair introduced his treatment of delict as follows:

"We come to the obligations by delinquences, which are civilly cognoscible by our custom, according to their known names and titles in our law; which, though they do rather signify the acts or actions, whereby such obligations are incurred or prosecuted, than the obligations themselves, yet they will be sufficient to hold out both. These are either general, having no particular name or designation: and such are pursued under the general name of damage and interest; which hath as many branches and specialties, as there can be valuable and reparable damages; besides those of a special name and nature, which are chiefly these, asythment, extortion, circumvention, defraud of creditors, spuilzie, intrusion, ejection, molestation, breach of arrestment, deforcement, contravention [of lawburrows], forgery..." (Stair, I, 9, 5.)

In this passage Stair does two things. First, he provides a general action for damage and interest. Secondly, he lists a number of specific wrongs, that is nominate delicts meaning delicts with names. The delicts listed are those operative in Scots law at that time, towards the end of the seventeenth century. A modern list of nominate delicts looks a little different. Assythment was abolished by the Damages (Scotland) Act 1976. Other delicts noted by Stair have become obscure, such as spuilzie, and contravention of lawburrows, while nominally part of the law, is seldom if ever pursued. A definitive and exhaustive list of nominate delicts remains elusive.

It has been argued strongly that Stair viewed the specific wrongs he listed as examples that could be subsumed under the general action. Another view is that Scots law operates with a general principle of reparation for loss wrongfully caused, plus a number of discrete delicts with their own rules for liability. When the true nature and structure of delict is considered there is scope for interpretation and debate. It is certainly clear, as Visser and Whitty state, that Stair presented the general action "in a way which made it compatible with the nominate delicts". It is also clear that there is a general principle of delictual liability and this serves to distinguish the underlying theoretical basis of Scots delict from its English equivalent, the law of torts.

Stair was ahead of his time in specifying the general action for damage and interest. He did, however, provide space for the law to develop and it is during the eighteenth century that we see the development of the general action in the context of liability for personal injury caused through unintentional, but nevertheless culpable, conduct. Specifically, the earliest cases were brought by pursuers who had been injured falling down holes that had been left in a state where there was no protection for the unwary pedestrian.

Damnum injuria datum

The *Lex Aquilia* of around 287 B.C. provided a penal action arising from the forcible destruction of certain types of property including the killing or wounding of slaves. The praetors (Roman magistrates) came to allow an action by analogy with the *Lex* in respect of property destruction caused indirectly and, by the time of the emperor Justinian in the sixth century A.D., Aquilian liability was stated in terms that covered all loss wrongfully caused.

Although Stair did not explicitly base the general action on Aquilian liability, it is clear that this civilian doctrine, especially as developed in Roman-Dutch law, was of great influence upon him. Pleadings in the earliest general action cases drew specifically upon the *Lex Aquilia*. Thus, the governing general principle of delictual liability in Scots law is said to be *damnum injuria datum*. This means loss (*damnum*) caused (*datum*) without legal justification (*injuria*) though it is common and helpful to read it as loss caused wrongfully.

Loss may be understood in terms of an infringement of a person's legal rights. In Scotland, we do not have a modern comprehensive and exhaustive statement of legally protected interests in the way that is found, for instance in German law (the German Civil Code, *Bürgerliches Gesetzbuch*, para.823). On the other hand, Stair provided a list of reparable or protected interests, the infringement of which covers most if not all forms of loss reparable in delict.

According to Stair (Stair, I, 4, 4), protected interests under the Scots law of delict are: (i) the right to life, members and health; (ii) the right to liberty; (iii) the right to fame, reputation and honour; (iv) the right to content, delight and satisfaction; and (v) the right to goods and possessions.

Thus personal injury or death is actionable in delict as is wrongful imprisonment and defamation. Damages in the form of solatium are recoverable for pain, suffering, inconvenience and affront. Damage to property is likewise reparable. The temporary invasion of a person's right to exclusive possession of property is not per se reparable, but may be remedied by interdict.

Stair's list of protected interests is not exhaustive. New protected interests may be added as a matter of policy. An example of a later addition to protected interests is the right to the comfortable enjoyment of property free from serious disturbance and substantial inconvenience. This right was first recognised in the common law of Scotland well after Stair's time and is protected by the doctrine of nuisance. Again, the commission of nuisance does not of itself give rise to a right to damages, but is remediable through interdict.

Loss, to be reparable, must be caused *injuria*; that is without legal justification or wrongfully. Loss that is not caused *injuria* is termed *damnum absque injuria* and is not reparable. In some instances the requirements of delict are satisfied because the act itself is unlawful. For example, where two or more parties conspire with the predominant purpose of injuring a person's business interests or where somebody knowingly induces one person to breach a contract with another. An act of trespass by walking across a person's ground is not in itself unlawful, but it may be an invasion of that person's right to exclusive possession so it will be an act committed *injuria*, unless, of course there is legal justification as in the case where statutory access rights are exercised. Disturbing or polluting activities are not necessarily unlawful, but may be regarded as such if they interfere with a neighbour's right to comfortable enjoyment of their own property to a degree sufficiently grave to amount in law to nuisance. In this instance an act becomes unlawful only because it invades another person's legally protected interest. Negligent acts are seldom unlawful or conducted without right—the wrong consists in the exercise of less care than is required by the circumstances so that the risk of harm to others materialises. Loss is a constituent element of delict so where there is a wrongful act, but no loss, that is *injuria sine damno,* there is no delict. Note however, that prospective harm may be prevented by interdict, for example in defamation or nuisance. Note also that loss does not always have to be tangible, in defamation affront or insult is adequate loss to trigger liability.

Culpa

The moral idea, that persons should only be held liable for losses for which they are to blame, is given legal expression in the principle that there should be no liability without fault. In Delict it is usual to use the Latin expression *culpa* for fault. In the nineteenth century in particular it was common to see the word *culpa* used as a synonym for negligence, this indeed is what it meant to the Romans, but in the modern formulation *culpa* is used as a generic term to embrace all forms of fault. Negligence then, is just a species of *culpa.*

There are exceptions to the no liability without fault rule, but these are thought now to be statutory exceptions only. Parliament is of course free to legislate that liability in particular circumstances should be strict. Where liability is strict this means that there is no requirement on the pursuer to show that the defender is at fault. Examples of strict liability imposed by statute may be found in Pt 1 of the Consumer Protection Act 1987 and s.1 of the Animals (Scotland) Act 1987.

Culpa then, is the essential basis for liability in reparation in Scots common law. In other words, no action at common law for delictual damages can succeed unless the pursuer proves *culpa* on the part of the defender. For much of the twentieth century it was argued that nuisance might be an exception, but since the House of Lords decision in *RHM Bakeries (Scotland) Ltd v Strathclyde Regional Council* it is clear *culpa* must be shown in an action for damages grounded on nuisance.

Culpa, as noted, is presently understood as a generic term under which can be brought all forms of fault. For many purposes it is sufficient to divide fault into two, fault is either intentional or unintentional. Unintentional fault is simply negligence. Intentional fault itself can be divided in two. Fault might be intentional in the sense that harm to the victim is intended. Equally, fault may be intentional in the sense that the wrongful act is deliberately done. In the latter case harm to the victim is unintended, but it is a more or less inevitable consequence of the deliberate act. So, it is culpable to do something deliberately which you know will have as a consequence, harm to another and it is also culpable to deliberately seek to harm another.

These two forms of intentional fault are recognised in the detailed consideration given to *culpa* by Lord President (as he then was) Hope in *Kennedy v Glenbelle*. Helpfully, in this model they are labelled differently so conduct intended to harm is denoted as malice and deliberate conduct where harm is an undesired, but inevitable consequence is denoted as intention. Lord Hope's presentation of the different forms taken by *culpa* is in the form of a continuum. At one end of the continuum is malice, where harm to the victim is the predominant objective of the act. Next to malice on the continuum is intention, meaning a deliberate act done in the knowledge that harm would be the result. Next along is recklessness, where harm to the pursuer is very likely, but the defender carries on regardless. At the foot of the continuum is negligence. In negligence there is a foreseeable risk of harm to the victim if the activity is carried out with insufficient care. Negligence consists in causing harm by taking insufficient care in circumstances where the law recognises a duty to exercise care. Negligence is differentiated from the other forms of *culpa* in this model on the basis that in negligence there is a risk of harm if sufficient care is not taken, whereas in the other categories harm is intended, inevitable or highly likely whether or not care is exercised.

Studying delict

By the standards of legal study delict is a relatively exciting subject. The authorities provide much material of historical, social and human interest. Civil liability offers a prism through which the interaction between law and the changing technological, social and indeed moral environments can be viewed. Although this text is intended to be useful at a basic level of undergraduate learning it is hoped that it does not altogether obscure the potential for intellectual challenge that the law of delict offers.

Some pointers can be offered the student who will soon be asked for his or her analysis of problems involving delictual liability. There are two crucial aspects of any scenario from which delictual liability may arise. These are: the nature of the loss or harm suffered or interest invaded and the circumstances in which the loss has occurred; and the presence or absence of fault and the form in which fault appears. These factors will indicate when a particular liability regime is applicable so, for example, where the interest invaded is reputation, liability in defamation is suggested; where loss is purely economic then there are particular rules that must be applied before liability in negligence can arise, but these rules will not apply where fault is intentional, for example where loss follows fraud. Where harm is caused by animals then you will refer for the rules on liability to the Animals (Scotland) Act 1987, although a common law case may also be possible. It is usually best to determine whether there is liability first, before considering whether there may be defences.

---

2. LIABILITY FOR NEGLIGENCE

INTRODUCTION

Negligence has been characterised as a failure to take care in circumstances where care is required. Not all harm caused carelessly, however, is reparable in law. Liability for negligence arises only in circumstances where the law recognises a duty to take care and foreseeable harm or loss results from the beach of that duty. It is best to avoid describing the duty of care as an obligation. The obligation to make reparation is only imposed once liability in negligence is established.

A clear example of a circumstance where the law imposes a duty of care is driving a vehicle. The act of driving always carries a risk of harm to others or their property if conducted without sufficient care. If X knocks Y off her bicycle, because X is looking at his passenger and not at the road, then X is negligent. X's negligence consists in causing Y injury through taking less care in the circumstances than he ought. Less care, that is, than would have been exercised by the reasonably careful driver in the circumstances. X will incur an obligation to make reparation; that is, X will be liable in damages for any injury Y suffers and for the cost of repairing or replacing Y's bike.

When a person embarks on an activity that is more or less certain to cause harm to others, irrespective of how much care is taken, this is culpable, but it is not negligent. In such circumstances *culpa* is better understood in terms of intention.

In the general case it is accepted that duties of care arise where the foreseeable risk is of injuring or killing persons and destroying or causing damage to their property. Other forms of harm, or specific circumstances may indicate particular liability regimes that must be applied. Where harm is psychiatric in nature or purely financial, liability may depend on the application of rules specific to these forms of harm. These are discussed in Chapters 3 and 4 respectively. Where harm results from a danger on premises over which the defender has control then analysis must proceed with reference to the Occupiers' Liability (Scotland) Act 1960. Where the harm is caused by animals then liability may arise under the Animals (Scotland) Act 1987, but that Act does not cover all forms of harm that may be done by any animal and so, depending on the circumstances, it may be relevant to consider liability at common law also.

SCOTS AND ENGLISH LAW

In English law negligence is both a tort in its own right and a means whereby another tort may be committed. The situation is different in Scots law. It has been argued that Scots law does not recognise a delict of negligence. Liability in negligence in Scots law can be seen as the application of the general principle of reparation, *damnum injuria datum*, in the context of unintentionally caused harm. In short, there is no delict of negligence in Scots law, but the law recognises liability for unintentional harm wrongfully caused on the basis of the general principle.

Liability for negligence in Scotland and England developed in different ways. Although the developing concept of duty of care may have been bringing the two jurisdictions closer together during the 19th century the major point of convergence occurred in 1932 in the celebrated case of *Donoghue v Stevenson*. This case concerned the delictual liability of a manufacturer to the ultimate consumer of his defective product. At the time, the English tort of negligence was somewhat inflexible, with courts only willing to recognise duties of care where there was a direct precedent for doing so. In an influential American case, *McPherson v Buick Motor Company*, the New York Court of Appeals opened up the potential for the liability of manufacturers to consumers in tort. Lord Atkin saw in *Donoghue*, a Scottish appeal to the House of Lords, an opportunity to open up English law in a similar fashion. He was assisted in doing so by the fact that counsel for both parties had conceded that, on the relevant points at issue, the laws of Scotland and England were the same. Lord Atkin, moreover, prevailed on one of the Scottish judges, Lord MacMillan to re-write his speech in terms of English rather than Scots law, thus ensuring that the lasting impact of the decision would apply not just in Scotland, but also in England and in those many jurisdictions in which English law is the major source of influence.

Lord Atkin formulated the neighbourhood principle which, by consolidating the concept of the duty of care and providing a basis for its recognition in very general terms, has facilitated much subsequent development of liability for negligence. Superficially at least, common law liability for negligence in Scotland looks very much like common law liability for negligence in England. The more important English cases are commonly cited in Scotland and the reverse is also true. It is best, however, to stop short of any assertion that the law is the same. A current state of affairs is not a warrant against future development and arguments that the law differs are sometimes possible. Important differences in theory and structure remain. In *A History of Private Law in Scotland*, Professors MacQueen and Sellar state:

> "[T]he intellectual superstructure of the law in the two systems remained different. Scots law held and continues to hold to the systematics of the law of obligations as laid down by Stair within the general tradition of the *jus commune*. Here there has been no shift

towards the common law. If anything, the shift has been in the other direction."

That said, the preponderance of new case law comes from England and, as negligence becomes increasingly complex, as the number of key decisions in which it becomes difficult to discern any uniform line of reasoning across the bench grows, as the areas of controversy and sometimes inconsistency seem to become greater, it becomes less easy to identify what systematics, if any, are being applied. The future of course is uncertain, but it could be that any distinctions in negligence are more likely to arise from the legislation of the Scottish Parliament rather than from development of the common law in the courts.

THE ANALYSIS OF NEGLIGENCE

It should be no surprise then that the analysis of negligence may differ when approached from a Scots or English perspective. This does not mean that there is an English analysis and a Scottish analysis; because negligence has become so complex it is becoming increasingly difficult to pin down any single analysis as representative of either jurisdiction. This, however, is a basic text and its purpose is to provide the reader who will be facing exams in the not too distant future with an easily navigated way into the subject. Negligence is presented here according to a simple structure. This is intended to make the basics of negligence easy to learn, it also provides a framework of understanding that may usefully be brought to bear on problem analysis in the exam hall. The reader who pursues their interest in delict may soon discover that differently structured presentations are possible, for example it is possible to provide an analysis that is not structured around the duty of care. The duty can be treated as a preliminary matter as Brian Pillans suggests, or it can be left to the end of the analysis as was done by Professor Bill Wilson. As every delict class has to be told, sometimes frequently, there is more than one way of skinning a cat and it is hoped that the structure employed here will provide some illumination at the introductory stages at least.

This presentation of negligence proceeds with a sequence of questions as follows: first, did the defender owe the pursuer a duty of care? Secondly, did the defender owe the pursuer a duty of care in respect of the harm that has arisen? Thirdly, did the defender breach the duty of care owed to the pursuer? Fourthly, was the defenders' breach the cause of the harm to the pursuer? Fifthly, should the defender compensate the pursuer for all losses?

THE DUTY OF CARE 1: Did the defender owe the pursuer a duty of care?

Duties may be imposed under particular statutory regimes. In the general case, where there is no applicable governing statute, it is necessary to determine liability according to the common law. The starting point is the case of *Donoghue v Stevenson*, in which the pursuer allegedly suffered severe gastro-enteritis after a decomposing snail emerged from an opaque bottle of "ginger" that she was pouring over her ice cream. This may have been ginger beer. Equally, the term "ginger" may have been used in the generic sense in which it is still used in the west of Scotland. Mrs Donoghue's stomach complaint arose from the fact she had already consumed some of the contents of the bottle.

Mrs Donoghue had no right of action in contract since she had no contract with the manufacturer. Moreover, she had no contract with the café owner since the drink had been bought for her by her friend. The House of Lords upheld the view of the Inner House that she had a relevant claim in delict. In a famous passage, Lord Atkin formulated what has become known as the neighbourhood principle:

> "The liability for negligence, whether you style it such or treat it as in other systems as a species of 'culpa', is no doubt based upon a general public sentiment of moral wrongdoing for which the offender must pay. But acts or omissions which any moral code would censure cannot, in a practical world, be treated so as to give a right to every person injured by them, to demand relief. In this way, rules of law arise which limit the range of complainants and the extent of their remedy. The rule that you are to love your neighbour becomes in law, you must not injure your neighbour; and the lawyer's question, Who is my neighbour? receives a restricted reply. You must take reasonable care to avoid acts or omissions which you can reasonably foresee would be likely to injure your neighbour. Who, then, in law, is my neighbour? The answer seems to be— persons who are so closely and directly affected by my act that I ought reasonably to have them in contemplation when I am directing my mind to the acts or omissions which are called into question."

A number of things can be seen from this dictum, one of which is that the rules on negligence are intended to keep liability within bounds. The need to restrict liability was felt less when delicts were generally intentional and potential victims were fewer. Once it was firmly established that delictual liability could arise from accidents then the need to avoid: "liability in an indeterminate amount for an indeterminate time, to an indeterminate class" became essential. This famous quote comes from Cardozo J. in *Ultramares Corporation v Touche*. Negligent acts are not intended to harm and justice requires some equation between the degree of culpability and the extent of liability.

The neighbourhood principle provides criteria by which a duty of care may be recognised. Duties of care are owed to our neighbours in law. These neighbours, then are the people whom we ought to have within our contemplation as being likely to be affected by our acts or omissions. In short, if X is doing something that entails a risk of harm to Y if X is not careful, then X is under a duty to take whatever precautions a reasonable person in the circumstances would take to guard against harm to Y. The neighbourhood principle does not, however, operate on its own. The neighbourhood principle tends to emphasise foreseeability, but foreseeability on its own is never enough. In addition there must be some element of proximity, bringing the pursuer within the contemplation of the defender. Thus, Y must be within the contemplation of X as being likely to be affected by X's activities. If X has no knowledge of Y and if there is no reason why X should have anticipated the existence of Y or anybody in the position of Y, then there is no duty owed. Duties of care are not owed to the whole world, it is not enough to say that a reasonable person ought to have contemplated that their conduct could have harmed somebody. Either the defender ought to have contemplated harm to the pursuer in particular or the defender ought to have contemplated harm to a sufficiently well defined class or group of persons of which the pursuer is a member.

The courts have developed the concept of proximity to limit the potential field of pursuers and to assist in determining whether defenders owed the pursuers duties of care. Proximity is an elusive concept when one tries to pin it down, but broadly it refers to factors that tend to draw the pursuer and defender closer so that it becomes easier to say that the defender ought to have had potential loss or harm to the pursuer within his or her contemplation. The key factor in *Donoghue* that supplied proximity was the fact that the drink was provided in an opaque bottle. Because of this, once it left the manufacturer's premises there was no opportunity for anyone to inspect it until it was opened by the consumer. This served to link the defender directly with the pursuer. Thus, the manufacturer and consumer were found to be in a proximate relationship whereby the defender ought to have had the consumer within his contemplation.

The simplest aspect of proximity is spacial or geographic. So, for instance, in *Bourhill v Young* the pursuer's case failed. A fishwife claimed that she had suffered nervous shock resulting in miscarriage when she heard the sound of a collision between a motorcycle and a car and later saw blood on the road. While it was accepted that the negligent motorcyclist owed a duty of care to other road users and pedestrians in the vicinity, Mrs Bourhill was at the far side of a tram when the accident occurred and was placed in no danger herself. The motorcyclist could not have foreseen injury to a pedestrian who was so far from events and so the action failed for lack of proximity. Mrs Bourhill herself was outwith the geographical area within which a duty of care was owed.

The idea of proximity is not, however, restricted to its spacial aspect. Proximity may be established by the defender's knowledge of the pursuer either as an individual or as a member of a well defined group or class, as in the cases where a duty is owed, because the defender is deemed to have assumed responsibility for the pursuer's interests. In *Gibson v Chief Constable of Strathclyde* police officers had been guarding a bridge which had collapsed. They had parked their Land Rover at one end of the bridge with the blue light flashing and the headlamps on so that anyone approaching from either end would be warned of the danger. Later, the officers left without being aware of whether any alternative warning had been established and the next vehicle to approach the bridge fell into the river, killing the driver and passenger. It was held that a duty of care was owed to the occupants of the vehicle. Having taken control of the situation the police officers were in a sufficiently proximate relationship with other users of that road for a duty to arise. More recently in *Burnett v Grampian Fire and Rescue Services* a duty of care was held to be owed by the defenders to those whose lives and property were endangered when they negligently failed to extinguish a fire properly. It re-ignited the following day causing extensive damage to the pursuer's flat.

Gibson and *Burnett* may be contrasted with the earlier English case of *Hill v Chief Constable of West Yorkshire*. The police had admitted to mistakes during their investigations into murders committed by serial killer Peter Sutcliffe, notorious as the "Yorkshire Ripper". Jacqueline Hill was Sutcliffe's final victim. Jacqueline's mother sued, alleging that the police were negligent in failing to identify and apprehend Sutcliffe prior to the murder of Jacqueline. The case was unsuccessful. While it was reasonably foreseeable to the police that young women in the Leeds area were in danger so long as Sutcliffe remained at large, no duty of care was owed to Jacqueline Hill in particular. There was nothing to alert the police to the danger that awaited Jacqueline as an individual and, as one woman in a large population, she was not within a sufficiently well defined class of persons for a duty to be owed her. There was no element of proximity to link the victim with the police so that she ought to have been within their contemplation.

The distinction between *Gibson* and *Hill* can be seen, at its simplest, in terms of whether the pursuers or claimants were within a sufficiently well defined class for a duty to be owed. Other differences lie in the different nature of the functions performed by police. There is a strong policy argument against civil liability arising from the investigation of crime. In these circumstances the responsible officers need to be free to make decisions according to their professional judgment without the constraint of having to guard against litigation. This argument does not have the same force when emergency services exercise a civil function in assuming control in hazardous road conditions.

While *Donoghue* has allowed for a duty of care to be recognised in a multiplicity of circumstances, in novel circumstances, that is where there is no direct precedent, the criteria for recognising a duty of care has been further developed.

A tripartite test was laid down by the House of Lords in *Caparo Industries plc v Dickman*. The three parts of the test are given equal weight. In order for a duty of care to be recognised, harm to the pursuer must be reasonably foreseeable; there must be a close degree of proximity between the parties; it must be fair, just and reasonable for the courts to recognise a duty. If any one of these three requirements is not satisfied there will be no duty.

This approach emphasises that foreseeability is not enough. It provides explicitly for an incremental approach to recognising duties of care in new circumstances. Rather than seeking to lay down general principles for liability the courts must consider factors tending either away from or towards proximity by applying to the present case proximity factors that have proved decisive in previously decided cases. In *Caparo* Lord Bridge cited with approval the following dictum of Brennan J. in the High Court of Australia in the case of *Sutherland Shire Council v Heyman*:

> "It is preferable, in my view, that the law should develop novel categories of negligence incrementally and by analogy with established categories, rather than by a massive extension of a prima facie duty of care restrained only by indefinable 'considerations which ought to negative, or reduce or limit the scope of the duty or the class of persons to whom it is owed.'"

The three part test provides an explicit role for policy considerations in the form of the fair just and reasonable requirement. In this way the court may decide that notwithstanding foreseeability and proximity it would be unjust to shift the loss from the pursuer to the defender. *Caparo* means that there must be some positive reason for imposing a duty of care. The test is generally applicable where the existence of a duty in novel situations is considered. The application of the *Caparo* requirements can be seen: in the context of personal injury in *Gibson v Chief Constable of Strathclyde* and *Mitchell v Glasgow City Council*; in the context of property harm in *Marc Rich & Co AG v Bishop Rock Marine Co Ltd*; and in the context of wrongful birth in *McFarlane v Tayside Health Board*. The *Caparo* test may be avoided where it appears, under *Henderson v Merrett* rules, that there has been an assumption of responsibility by the defender. This point is discussed in Chapter 3 below.

THE DUTY OF CARE 2: Did the defender owe the pursuer a duty of care in respect of the harm that has arisen?

The focus in the previous section was to whom duties are owed. In this section we consider the scope of the duty, that is, in respect of what is the duty owed. The duty of care involves the requirement to guard against risks that are likely to materialise, but not against all eventualities. One is only liable for the foreseeable consequences that a reasonable person in the position of the defender would have contemplated as probable in the circumstances.

This point may be demonstrated by reference to the House of Lords decision in the Scottish case of *Muir v Glasgow Corporation*. Participants in a Sunday school picnic in King's Park, Glasgow, sought shelter from the rain in a tea-room run by the Glasgow Corporation. The corporation's employee on the premises, Mrs Alexander, gave permission for the picnic and allowed an urn full of boiling water to be carried down a passageway to the tea-room. One of the two persons carrying the urn dropped his handle and several children who were queuing to buy sweets were scalded. The corporation was sued in negligence.

It was held that the spillage was not foreseeable as a reasonable and probable consequence of Mrs Alexander's conduct in allowing the urn to be carried. She was entitled to assume that the carriers would have been reasonably careful.

It follows that, if X can foresee personal injury as the probable consequence of his throwing bricks over a wall, he will be liable if he fails to take reasonable precautions and Y is injured. If personal injury is foreseeable, but property harm is not and Y has left his property behind the wall and it is damaged, then X is not likely to be liable.

The difficulty in analysis is that there are two different ways of looking at this issue. It can be considered in terms of the duty itself or in terms of breach of the duty. In *Muir*, Lord Macmillan took the view that no duty was owed the children in respect of the improbable and unforeseeable event which occurred. This is a logically defensible position with the advantage that it is easily explained. Examples of this reasoning can be found in later cases, for example in *Caparo Industries v Dickman* the negligent auditors were held to have owed a statutory duty to existing shareholders as members of the company, but they owed no duty to those same shareholders as potentials purchasers of further shares. As it becomes increasingly recognised that issues of duty, causation and remoteness are intertwined with one another and as the scope of duties is given ever increasing scrutiny it could be that this approach will become the one that is favoured.

The second way of looking at the same issue is the more commonly accepted. In this view the issue is approached, not as a question of duty, but a question of the requisite care to be taken if the duty is not to be breached. In *Muir*, in contrast to Lord Macmillan, Lords Thankerton, Wright, and Romer all found that a duty was owed, but it was not breached. The point being that the duty is to take reasonable care to guard against those risks that are most likely to materialise. So long as the defender has acted reasonably in respect of foreseeable risks there is no breach and no liability. The duty may be fulfilled where sufficient precautions are taken to guard against foreseeable risks, but risks that are present, but improbable, may, perhaps, be ignored by the reasonably careful party.

As Lord Oaksey explained:

> "The standard of care in the law of negligence is the standard of an ordinary careful man, but in my opinion an ordinary careful man does not take precautions against every foreseeable risk. He can, of course, foresee the possibility of many risks, but life would be almost impossible if he were to attempt to take precautions against every risk which he can foresee. He takes precautions against risks which are reasonably likely to happen. Many foreseeable risks are extremely unlikely to happen and cannot be guarded against except by almost complete isolation."

The context for these remarks was the English House of Lords case of *Bolton v Stone*. In that case a cricket ball was struck right out of a cricket ground where it injured a person around 100 yards from the wicket. While the event was foreseeable, balls had been struck out of the ground six times in the previous 30 years, the defendants who operated the cricket ground were not obliged to have guarded against it. The risk of injury was so remote that a reasonable person would not have anticipated it. *Bolton v Stone* may be contrasted with the case of *Lamond v Glasgow Corporation* in which a golf ball was hit onto a footpath where it struck the pursuer on the head. In that case the duty of care was breached since the event was not only possible, but also probable. It was established in evidence that on average 6,000 golf balls were played onto the footpath every year, although there was no previously reported instance of anybody having been struck.

Care must be taken with the view that risks which are foreseeable, but improbable may be ignored. In reference to *Bolton*, Lord Reid, in *The Wagon Mound (No. 2)* explained that there must be some valid reason for ignoring the risk, for example the expense or inconvenience of guarding against the risk. The question is whether a reasonable man, careful of the safety of his neighbour, would think it right to neglect the risk. This point is considered further below under breach of duty.

The House of Lords decision in *Hughes v Lord Advocate* demonstrates a very important point. Although the precise way in which an accident occurs may not be reasonably foreseeable, if some accident of that type or general nature is foreseeable then liability may be established. This case involved a hole in the road, covered with a tent, but otherwise insufficiently guarded. Boys investigated with a paraffin lamp that had been marking the road works. The lamp was knocked down the hole, the paraffin vaporised and ignited causing an explosion that burned one of the boys badly. It was held that the explosion was not foreseeable. However, it was foreseeable that a child might enter the tent with a lamp, that paraffin might spill and that the child might be burned. Therefore the duty of care owed to pedestrians was breached.

Similarly in *Wilson v Chief Constable of Lothian and Borders Police* a man died of hypothermia having been released by police in a drunken condition in an isolated place at 5.45 on a January morning. It had been snowing heavily, the temperature was 0°C. The body was found a week later over two miles from the site of release. It was held that the police were not bound to have foreseen the man's death from hypothermia, but they should have foreseen that he would be exposed to various risks of severe harm. They were under a particular duty to have regard to the reasonably foreseeable consequences of his release. The officers concerned had failed to direct their minds to the likely consequences of their act and had exposed the deceased to unnecessary risk. The chain of events that was foreseeable was not different in kind from those that led to his death.

The rule, that one is only liable for foreseeable consequences, is subject to an exception in personal injury cases. Here, the defender takes his victim as he finds him. Thus, in *McKillen v Barclay-Curle*, the negligent defender who was liable for the pursuer's fractured rib was also liable for the consequent reactivation of the pursuer's tuberculosis, even though this could not have been foreseen by the defender.

BREACH OF DUTY. Did the defender breach the duty of care owed to the pursuer?

Establishing a duty of care is only the first step in an action based on negligence. Next it has to be established that the duty was breached. This raises the issue, how much care was the defender obliged to exercise? The defender will only be liable to make reparation if it can be shown that the care taken was less than that required by law. In other words the defender's conduct must have fallen short of that necessary to fulfil the duty. The abstract concept of duty of care is given content by the standard of care. It is up to pursuers to stipulate exactly what the duty was, what the defender should have or should not have done, and to specify the way in which their conduct deviated from the standard required.

The standard of care imposed by law is that of the reasonable man, or ordinarily careful person. So a defender will only be liable if their conduct showed less care than would have been exercised by a reasonable person in the position of the defender at the time at which the event occurred. The standard of the reasonable man is an objective standard and courts will not enquire too deeply into the idiosyncrasies of the individual. Thus *Nettleship v Weston* establishes that a learner driver owes the same standard of care to other road users as an experienced driver. If this seems harsh on the learner driver, the point is that other road users and pedestrians are entitled to expect a certain degree of care, not differing standards according to the experience or lack of it of the driver.

It is important to note that the standard of care is a flexible concept. The degree of care required by law varies according to the circumstances. As Lord MacMillan stated in *Muir v Glasgow Corporation*, "[t]here is no absolute standard, but it may be said generally that the degree of care required varies directly with the risk involved". Some activities require a level of care that is little more than mundane, for example, applying the handbrake when parking a car. Other activities require the most elaborate precautions, open heart surgery or nuclear fission, for example.

The point was put well by Lord Neaves in *Mackintosh v Mackintosh*: "[n]o prudent man in carrying a lighted candle through a powder magazine would fail to take more care than if he was going through a damp cellar".

Ultimately, courts will determine what precautions a reasonable person in the defender's position ought to take or the level of care that ought to be exercised. This determination has been assisted by the identification of factors that ought to be taken into consideration in assessing risk. The most relevant considerations are the likelihood of the risk of harm materialising and the magnitude of the harm if the risk does materialise. This aspect of the law of negligence may be explained most clearly in the context of accidents at work, a situation in which the existence of a duty of care is clear.

It has been held that there is a duty on employers to weigh on the one hand, the magnitude of risk, the likelihood of an accident happening and the possible gravity of any accident against, on the other hand, the difficulty, expense and disadvantage of taking any particular precaution. This balancing process is termed "the calculus of risk". While these factors derive from the judgment of Lord Reid in *Morris v West Hartlepool Steam Navigation Co Ltd* and are commonly illustrated by reference to other employment cases, the basic approach of weighing up the risks against the practicability of precautions is not restricted to the employment field.

In *Brisco v Secretary of State for Scotland* a prison officer sought damages of £2,000 in respect of a broken bone in his little toe, sustained when a heavy fence post thrown from above landed on him during a simulated riot. The pursuer contended that his employers were in breach of their duty to him in failing to issue an instruction forbidding the throwing of heavy objects. In the Inner House the factors outlined in the previous paragraph were considered. In the light of the need for riot training of prison officers under realistic circumstances the instruction contended for by the pursuer would have amounted to a disadvantage. This disadvantage was sufficient to outweigh the relatively slight risk involved. Accordingly there was no breach of duty.

In *Latimer v AEC Ltd* a factory floor became slippery after flooding. Three tons of sawdust was put down on the floor, but the plaintiff slipped on an uncovered part of the floor and was injured. He argued that the factory should have been closed down. The House of Lords held that the employer had done all that a reasonable employer would have done. Closing down the factory would have meant a loss of production, and the expense and disadvantage of this was not outweighed by the relatively small danger to which the plaintiff had been exposed.

A further means of contending for a particular standard of care is to show that defenders have not followed usual practice. The House of Lords decision in *Brown v Rolls Royce* demonstrates that failure to adopt a normal practice is not conclusive proof of negligence, but merely a fact from which negligence may be inferred. The plaintiff contracted dermatitis. He was a machine oiler whose hands were constantly in contact with oil. Evidence was led to show that it was common practice for employers to provide Rozalex #1, a barrier cream. Rolls Royce had not done so, but they had sought medical advice on the issue and contended that Rozalex was not an effective prophylactic. They had made alternative provision in the form of adequate washing facilities. Rolls Royce was not in breach. They had not neglected to take precautions, but had considered the issue, made provision and had demonstrated the conduct and judgment of a reasonable employer. Thus, normal practice may be of evidential value, but will not, in itself, determine the issue.

In *Paris v Stepney Borough Council* it was not at the time usual practice to supply goggles to employees doing the work of the plaintiff. However, this employee had been blinded in one eye during the war. When he lost his sight completely through an accident at work that would have been prevented had he been supplied with goggles, his employers were held in breach of their duty to him. This is an example in which the potential magnitude of harm is great given special attributes of the individual owed a duty. Accordingly, a standard of care which is higher than that which operates for other individuals is justified.

CAUSATION: Was the defender's breach the cause of harm to the pursuer?

It is necessary to show that the harm complained of resulted from the defender's breach. A causal link must be established. It must be shown by the pursuer that "but for" the breach, the loss would not have occurred. Thus in *McWilliams v Sir William Arrol & Co* employers were in breach of their duty since they failed to provide a steel erector with a safety belt. However, they were not liable when he plunged to his death since it was established in evidence that, even if he had been given a belt, the steel erector would not have worn it. It could not be said that "but for" the defenders' breach the pursuer would not have been injured. Similarly in *McKinlay v British Steel Corporation* the pursuer claimed that he had not been instructed and encouraged to wear safety goggles in accordance with the duty on the defenders. On the evidence it was held that the pursuer had failed to establish that he would have worn goggles if instructed to do so. The defenders were assoilzied. In *Barnett v Chelsea and Kensington Hospital Management Committee* the casualty officer was in breach of duty in failing to see a patient who presented with violent vomiting. The patient died later of arsenic poisoning. The hospital was not liable despite the breach, because it was established that the patient would have died anyway. His death was not attributable to the doctor's breach of duty.

So the breach must be the factual cause of the loss. This is expressed as the *causa sine qua non*. This is a necessary, but not sufficient basis for establishing causation. In order to establish causation it is also necessary to establish that the breach is the *causa causans*; that is the breach must be the legal cause in the sense of being the effective, dominant or immediate cause. Of course, in many circumstances the factual and legal cause are the same and the issue only arises where there are complications in the causal chain. Such complications arise, for example, where there are further acts by the pursuer or by third parties which have some effect on the victim.

The difficulties associated with causation have been exercising the minds of lawyers for a rather long time. This is illustrated by the following passage from Roman law that will enable the distinction between *causa sine qua non* and *causa causans* to be illustrated.

> "Celsus writes that if one attacker inflicts a mortal wound on a slave and another person later finishes him off, he who struck the earlier blow will not be liable for a killing, but for wounding, because he actually perished as a result of another wound." (D.9.2.11.3.)

The original wound is a *causa sine qua non*, since "but for" the wound the slave might not have been lying around in a position where he could be wounded again. So the original wound is the factual cause. However, the original wound is not the *causa causans*. The *causa causans* is the second attack that kills the slave. The second attack is the effective, dominant or immediate cause of death. The second attack is a *novus actus interveniens* (new act intervening) which breaks the chain of causation between the infliction of the original wound and death, relieving the original wrongdoer from liability. An event which is a probable consequence of the original act will not break the causal chain. A *novus actus interveniens* is some unpredictable event which does not follow naturally as a probable or foreseeable consequence of the *causa sine qua non*. As Lord Wright expressed it in *The Oropesa*:

> "To break the chain of causation it must be shown that there is something which I will call ultroneous, something unwarrantable, a new cause which disturbs the sequence of events, something which can be described as either unreasonable or extraneous or extrinsic. I doubt whether the law can be stated more precisely than that."

Thus in *Fraser v Bell* a ferocious dog jumped on a coalman who dropped his sack on the foot of another man. The party responsible for the dog was liable for the injured foot. Dropping the sack was an involuntary act, the natural consequence of the attack and not a *novus actus interveniens* breaking the chain of causation. Similarly in *Scott v Shepherd* a person who threw a lighted firework into a crowd was liable for the injuries it caused even though two persons had picked it up and thrown it on before it finally exploded. The acts of throwing the firework on were probable consequences of the original act.

In *McKew v Holland & Hannon & Cubitts (Scotland) Ltd* the pursuer injured his ankle as a result of the defenders' negligence. His leg thereafter was liable to "give way" on occasions. After the accident he went to visit a flat. Access to the flat was by way of a stair with no handrail. The pursuer descended the stairway without care, his leg gave way, he panicked and jumped down 10 steps causing injury to his other leg. The court held the defenders liable for the original injury, but not the second. By descending the stairs without care the pursuer's own act constituted a *novus actus interveniens*. The defenders' breach was a *causa sine qua non* of the second injury, but it was not the *causa causans*.

A further complicating factor arises where there may be more than one cause for the harm suffered. In *Wardlaw v Bonnington Castings* the pursuer contracted pneumoconiosis from breathing in dust at work. The dust might have come from the hammer that he operated, for which there was no known means of providing protection and therefore no breach of duty on the part of the employers. Equally the dust might have come from grinders and other machinery for which protection could have been, but was not, provided. Accordingly, the employers were not in breach in respect of one possible source, but were in breach in respect of the other. The House of Lords held that the pursuer could succeed in negligence if he could show that dust from the source for which the defenders were in breach had materially contributed to his injuries. In this case the "but for" test was relaxed.

In *Wardlaw* the potential sources of harm operated concurrently. In the subsequent House of Lords case of *McGhee v National Coal Board* the point was extended to cover sources operating consecutively. In that case also there were two possible sources of harm, one of which involved breach of duty and the other did not. The pursuer worked in a kiln and was exposed to dust. There was no means of effecting protection and therefore no breach of duty. The defenders had failed to supply washing facilities which was a breach of duty and so the pursuer cycled home from work everyday in a generally dusty condition. Again it was impossible to determine whether it was the exposure to dust or the lack of washing facilities that was the effective cause of the pursuer's dermatitis. The pursuer may have contracted dermatitis purely through his work or it might have been that there would have been no harm had he been able to clean up before going home. In this case the "but for" test was abandoned altogether and it was held that the pursuer could succeed if the breach had materially contributed to the *risk* of harm.

In *Fairchild v Glenhaven Funeral Services* the House of Lords developed further the law on causation. The pursuer contracted mesothelioma as a consequence of exposure to asbestos dust. The complicating factor in this case was that he had been exposed to asbestos while working for two different employers at different times and over different periods. Both parties were in breach, but it was impossible to attribute the source of the disease to a particular employer or a particular period of employment. In this case the "but for" test was suspended. Since the risk of mesothelioma increases with total exposure to asbestos, both employers had materially contributed to the risk and both were found jointly and severally liable.

The net effect of developments since *Fairchild* has been to leave to law in the same position, at least where the injury suffered is mesothelioma. In *Barker v Corus* the House of Lords departed from *Fairchild*. The claimant had been exposed to three sources of asbestos at different times. For one of these he was himself responsible as he was self-employed at the time. The decision was that each defender was liable only in proportion to the magnitude of the risk of injury to which it had exposed the claimant. The effect of this ruling is that liability is divisible rather than joint and several in cases of risk creation. This decision was effectively reversed by the Compensation Act 2006, s.3 of which applies in Scotland. This Act reinstates joint and several liability while making further provision for the apportionment of contributions between defenders and moreover retains the possibility of reduction in damages for contributory negligence.

It appears that where there are two potential sources of harm from the same noxious agent, a material increase in risk may be treated as a material contribution and causation may be established on this basis. The sources need not operate concurrently. Where more than one party is responsible for the material increase in risk all parties in breach may be found liable. Where the harm suffered is not mesothelioma then presumably *Barker* should be followed and liability apportioned according to the degree of risk to which each defender exposed the pursuer. Where the harm is mesothelioma then liability is governed by the Compensation Act 2006.

REMOTENESS OF DAMAGE: Should the defender compensate the
pursuer for all losses?

Where loss occurs there may be no end to the consequences. Imagine X is
knocked off her motorbike by the negligence of a car driver while on her
way to a job interview. X can seek reparation in respect of her physical
injuries both in terms of pain and suffering and any disability sustained.
But X's loss does not end there. Because X is in hospital when she was
scheduled to be at the interview, she does not get the new job and has to
continue in her present job that pays far less. Her family suffers financially
and eventually her marriage breaks down due to financial strains. Such
losses would be regarded as too speculative to be reparable. After all, she
may have failed the interview.

A line has to be drawn somewhere between consequences which the
negligent defender must bear and those which must be borne by the victim.
Thus we have the concept of remoteness of damage, the law will not
compensate damage that is too remote. It may be noted that, depending on
the approach taken by the court, the same issue — for which losses should
the defender compensate? — may be determined at another stage by
considering the scope of the duty or may indeed be resolved in terms of
causation. See for example, Lord Hoffman's speech in *South Australia
Asset Management Corporation v York Montague Ltd*. An analysis of
negligence which presents these elements as discrete is becoming less
reflective of the way in which courts actually proceed.

Historically there has been some difficulty in identifying the criteria
applied in Scots law to determine which losses are too remote. It is common
to cite a dictum of Lord Kinloch in *Allan v Barclay*:

> "The grand rule on the subject of damages is that none can be
> claimed except such as naturally and directly arise out of the wrong
> done; and such therefore, as may reasonably be supposed to have
> been in the view of the wrongdoer."

This equates direct consequences with those that are reasonably
foreseeable. In the past this has caused some difficulty since in English
cases direct and reasonably foreseeable consequences have been
distinguished and there is conflicting authority to support either view. In *Re
Polemis v Furness Withy & Co Ltd* the Court of Appeal unequivocally
rejected foreseeability as the test whereas in *Overseas Tankship (UK) Ltd
v Morts Dock and Engineering Co Ltd (The Wagon Mound)* the Privy
Council rejected the *Polemis* approach, holding that, in order to be
recoverable, the damage had to be a reasonably foreseeable consequence of
the defendant's negligence.

The matter appears to have been resolved, for Scots law anyway, in an
appeal to the House of Lords in a Scottish case, *Simmons v British Steel plc*.
Lord Rodger summarised the law in five points. Strictly speaking only the
first (and perhaps the fourth) point deals with remoteness *per se*, but this

summary acknowledges implicitly that rules on remoteness do not operate in isolation to place limits on the scope of the defender's liability.

1. Once liability is established in terms of duty and breach the starting point is that the defender is not to be held liable for consequences that are not reasonably foreseeable.
2. However, the defender is not necessarily liable for all consequences that are reasonably foreseeable. Depending on circumstances there may be no liability for harm resulting from a *novus actus interveniens*, or from unreasonable conduct by the pursuer even if that was foreseeable.
3. Subject to [rules on causation] point 2 above, there will be liability for harm of a kind that was foreseeable even though the harm is greater than could have been foreseen or where it was caused in a way that could not have been foreseen, as, for example, in *Hughes v Lord Advocate*.
4. Subject to [rules on causation] point 2 above, the defender takes his victim as he finds him, so, for example, in *McKillen v Barclay Curle* liability was established not only in respect of the pursuer's fractured rib, but also for consequent reactivation of the pursuer's tuberculosis which the defender could not have foreseen.
5. Subject to [rules on causation] point 2 above, where personal injury is a foreseeable consequence of negligence the defender is liable whether the injury is physical or psychiatric, as in *Page v Smith* discussed below in Ch.4.*Simmons v British Steel plc* makes clear that the governing criteria on remoteness of damage is foreseeability, while noting in point 2 that even foreseeable consequences may not be reparable where there has been a break in the chain of causation. There remains much scope for flexibility and argument. The line to be drawn between losses that are reparable and those that are merely speculative will vary according to the circumstances of the particular case but, generally speaking, losses that are speculative will not be compensated. In the example given at the start of this section, the motorcyclist will not recover damages for losses arising from her failure to get the new job.

A note of caution may be added. In limited circumstances it may be possible to obtain damages in respect of loss of a chance. Thus in *Kyle v P&J Stormonth-Darling WS* a firm of solicitors was held liable in damages to its client for failing to lodge appeal papers. It was by no means certain that the client would have won the appeal, but loss in such circumstances can be seen in terms of the loss of a legal right. This is similar in principle to the earlier English case of *Kitchen v Royal Air Force*. In England loss of a chance to make an economic gain due to negligent misstatement has been relevant in some cases such as *Allied Maples Group Ltd v Simmons and Simons*. In *Gregg v Scott* the House of Lords by a majority rejected a claim based on reduced chances of recovery from cancer where treatment had been delayed, because of an earlier misdiagnosis. The delay reduced this chance from 42% to 25% so even without misdiagnosis the claimant always had a less than evens chance.

LIABILITY FOR THE ACTS OF THIRD PARTIES

Outwith circumstances in which vicarious liability operates, one is in general not liable for the deliberate acts of third parties. Normally any such act would constitute a *novus actus interveniens* breaking the chain of causation between the defender's breach and the pursuer's loss. Liability in negligence in such circumstances is very much the exception rather than the rule.

In *Dorset Yacht Co v Home Office* the House of Lords found in favour of the owners of a yacht damaged when borstal boys under the control of prison officers attempted to escape from an island in Poole harbour. Critical to the decision was the view that the prison officers had a supervisory role over the boys, some of whom had a record of absconding, and the escape ought to have foreseen. Since the officers knew of the presence of the yacht and that the yacht offered the only feasible means of escape, they should have foreseen the events that transpired. The boys escaped, commandeered the yacht and there was a collision. The officers owed a duty of care to the owners of the yacht since they ought to have foreseen harm to their property as the result of the negligent way in which they exercised their supervisory role. They had gone to bed and left the boys to their own devices.

This case can be seen as an extension of the duty of care to cover acts by third parties, but it can be rationalised, as Lord Reid did in his speech, in terms of causation. An act of a third party need not necessarily be seen as a *novus actus interveniens*, especially where, in a case such as this, the third party is under the control of the negligent party. Even though the harm occurred through voluntary actions on the part of the boys, these actions were foreseeable as a probable consequence of the prison officers' negligence.

Liability for the acts of third parties has also been considered in the context of whether there is a duty owed to neighbours in respect of damage caused by persons entering the pursuer's property. In *Evans v Glasgow DC* the neighbourhood principle from *Donoghue* was applied to hold landlords liable for property damage in a tenement caused by vandals who had entered via adjoining vacant property. The defenders were negligent in failing to secure the vacant property against a foreseeable risk. In 1986 the case of *Squires v Perth & Kinross District Council* was determined in the Inner House. The second defender, a firm of building contractors, was found liable in negligence having breached a duty of care owed to the pursuers to secure premises against access by third parties. The builders had been carrying out renovation work on flats above the pursuers' premises, a jewellers shop. A thief had gained access to one of the flats which was not properly secured and had broken through the floor into the shop below. The court held that this was an event that ought to have been foreseen and guarded against. As Lord Wheatley said, "[a]ny reasonable person in occupancy and control would have foreseen the likelihood of what in fact occurred".

It may be noted that liability in the three cases discussed above was imposed in respect, not of positive acts, but of omissions. The law will not normally impose liability in respect of a pure omission so, for example, if X sees that Y is in danger of drowning X will not be liable if he does not throw Y a lifeline and Y drowns. Omissions, on the other hand may be treated the same as acts, but only where a positive duty to act is recognised so X may be liable if he omits to maintain the brakes on his lorry where a duty of care is recognised that he should do so. A key element in recognising a duty in *Dorset Yacht Co* was the fact that the prison officers had control over the boys who were likely, if uncontrolled, to cause damage. This element of control over the wrongdoers is lacking in *Evans* and *Squires*, duties seem to have been recognised purely on grounds of foreseeability of harm. The modern approach to duties of care emphasises that foreseeability is not enough and, in the context of any duty to secure premises against third parties this appears affirmed, not without ambiguity, in *Maloco v Littlewoods* (also reported sub nom. *Smith v Littlewoods*). The defenders owned an empty cinema, the Regal, in Dunfermline. Children broke in and started fires which damaged neighbouring property. The House of Lords held that there was no breach of any duty owed to neighbouring proprietors.

Lord McKay, a Scottish judge, appeared to determine the case on the ground that the event that transpired was not foreseeable. The defenders did not know of previous acts of vandalism involving fire. Since the cinema was not an obvious fire risk the defenders were not under a duty to anticipate the possibility of fire by vandals.

The decision in *Maloco* may, however be better explained as following the English Court of Appeal case of *Perl Exporters v Camden LBC*. In that case the defendants were held to owe no duty to neighbours to secure their property, despite the fact that they had been made well aware of the accessibility of the property to vagrants and of the concerns of the plaintiffs regarding security. When thieves broke through the adjoining wall and stole garments belonging to the plaintiffs, Perl sued in negligence. Notwithstanding the manifest carelessness of the defendants it was held that no duty of care was owed.

Lord Goff stated:

> "Is every occupier of a terraced house under a duty to his neighbours to shut his windows or lock his door when he goes out, or to keep access to his cellars secure, or even to remove his fire escape, at the risk of being held liable in damages if thieves thereby obtain access to his own house and thence to his neighbour's house? I cannot think that the law imposes any such duty."

Lord Goff demonstrates the English reluctance to recognise a duty of care in respect of a pure omission. The extent to which Scots law differs in this respect may be arguable. Clearly, English law imposes no duty on proprietors to secure their property against third parties even though it is foreseeable that such persons may use their access to the property to cause harm to neighbouring properties. In *Perl* and *Maloco* it was not any positive act on the part of the defending parties that was complained of, but a failure to act in circumstances where the law recognises no duty to act.

An argument, that Scots and English law differ on omissions met with no success in *Mitchell v Glasgow City Council*. Mitchell was a council tenant who had had problems with a neighbour, Drummond, over some six years. This had started in December 1994 when Mitchell complained to Drummond about noise. Drummond had battered Mitchell's door with an iron bar, smashed windows and threatened to kill Mitchell after the police had become involved. Such events continued to happen on a regular basis. Drummond was called to a meeting with the council in which he was threatened with eviction in July 2001. Following this meeting Drummond killed Mitchell with an iron bar. An action was raised in which it was contended that the council was negligent in failing to warn Mitchell that this meeting was taking place. The House of Lords applied *Caparo* rules to hold that no such duty was owed at common law. It was also held that the council was not in breach of its positive duty under ECHR Art.2 to protect life since there was no reason to apprehend any immediate threat to Mitchell's life.

WRONGFUL BIRTH AND CONCEPTION

Within the last 20 years there has been a number of actions brought against doctors and their employers in respect of the birth of unplanned or unwanted children. The general tendency has been to admit such claims.

Such a claim may arise from the failure of hospital staff to warn a pregnant mother of potential physical or mental impairment in the foetus so that the mother is denied the opportunity to terminate the pregnancy. This is wrongful birth. It is established that a duty of care to inform the mother is owed in such circumstances. If the duty is breached, damages will be recoverable. The Scots case of *McLelland v Greater Glasgow Health Board* follows the earlier decision of the Court of Appeal in *McKay v Essex Area Health Authority*.

Another way in which such claims arise is where a sterilisation has been performed negligently or, more pertinently, where the patient has been negligently informed that the operation has been a success when it was not. This is wrongful conception. Unwanted pregnancy and childbirth is held to be reparable loss.

While the moral aspects of regarding the birth of a child as a loss provide scope for discussion, the legal point with which we are concerned here is the extent of the duty owed the parents. This was ruled upon by the House of Lords in the case of *McFarlane v Tayside Health Board*. In *McFarlane* the male pursuer, a father of four, underwent a vasectomy and was subsequently given the "all clear" whereas in fact the operation had been unsuccessful. Subsequently his wife conceived a fifth child. The McFarlanes sued, seeking solatium in respect of pain, suffering and inconvenience consequential on pregnancy and childbirth and damages in respect of the financial costs of bringing up the child.

At first instance the Lord Ordinary, Lord Gill, accepted that a duty of care was owed to the parents, but refused to countenance either the birth of a healthy child as a reparable loss or pregnancy and childbirth as personal injury. On reclaiming, the Second Division reversed this decision. Unplanned conception was held to amount to a loss and the McFarlanes were awarded both solatium and damages in respect of financial costs of upbringing.

The defenders appealed to the House of Lords on the basis that natural processes of conception and childbirth could not in law amount to personal injury. This argument was rejected and the mother's claim for solatium was allowed by a majority (Lord Millet dissenting). It was accepted, therefore, that unplanned conception amounted to a wrong. However, the claim for financial costs was rejected unanimously. While a duty of care was owed in respect of avoiding pregnancy the Court determined that it would not be fair, just and reasonable to extend the scope of this duty to cover the financial costs of raising the child. In short, as it has been put by one commentator, "doctors and the NHS are not to pay for the upbringing of healthy children".

The question that arose following *McFarlane*, in which the child was born healthy, was whether damages would be recoverable for the costs of upbringing in the event that a child was born with some impairment. In *McLelland v Greater Glasgow Health Board* damages were awarded in respect of the extra costs of maintenance attributable to mental impairment. However, this does not answer the point since in this case the wrong consisted of a negligent failure to diagnose mental impairment *in utero*, thus denying the mother the choice of whether to proceed with the pregnancy. Subsequently, in *Parkinson v St James and Seacroft University NHS Trust* the claimant was awarded damages in the Court of Appeal, not for the basic costs of upbringing, but for the extra costs of raising an autistic child. This was a case of negligently performed sterilisation and therefore wrongful conception, but *Parkinson* has since been followed in *Farraj v King's Healthcare NHS Trust*, in which a misdiagnosis *in utero* wrongly excluded a blood disorder. It may be that there is no useful distinction to be drawn between wrongful birth and conception.

Subsequent to *Parkinson*, in a further wrongful conception case *Rees v Darlington Memorial Hospital*, the Court of Appeal awarded a mother damages in respect of the extra costs, consequent upon the mother's visual impairment, of bringing up a healthy child. This decision was reversed in the House of Lords. Ultimately the mother was awarded damages in respect of pregnancy and childbirth as per *McFarlane*. In addition she was awarded a "conventional sum" of £15,000. This sum is awardable in all cases where birth follows failed sterilisation. The conventional payment is itself controversial. *Rees*, like *McFarlane*, was determined on a majority. The issues remain highly controversial and the law should not yet be regarded as fully settled.

DEFENCES

In general the pursuer's pleadings may be attacked at any point. In defence it may be argued that: no duty of care was owed the pursuer; the appropriate standard of care was exercised; the alleged harm was not caused by the pursuer; the alleged loss was too remote. Note that the facts averred by the pursuer may also be challenged. The defender may be able to establish in proof a very different version of events. The defender may challenge the extent of harm averred by the pursuer.

Over and above any such attack on fundamental aspects of the pursuer's case, the defender may argue that the pursuer contributed to their losses. This is a plea of contributory negligence. In personal injury cases such a plea is more or less routine. It must be established that the pursuer was at fault in that their act or omission fell below the standard of a reasonable person in the pursuer's position. A common example is where a passenger in a car is injured as a result of the driver's negligence, but injuries are exacerbated because the passenger has failed to wear a seatbelt.

The effect of a successful plea of contributory negligence is to reduce the sum payable in damages by an amount to reflect the degree of the pursuer's own contribution to the harm sustained (Law Reform (Contributory Negligence) Act 1945 s.1). Prior to the 1945 Act contributory negligence was a complete defence, exonerating the defender entirely from the obligation to make reparation.

Where contribution is established, courts apportion blame for the damage between the parties and seek to effect a reduction in damages that is just and equitable. For example, in *Sayers v Harlow UDC* damages were reduced by 25 per cent to reflect the plaintiff's own contribution to her injuries. She had been trapped in a public toilet cubicle, but in attempting to climb out was held to have contributed to her losses. Her foot slipped on the toilet roll holder and she fell to the floor.

In reducing damages courts must determine the total damages that would have been awarded had there been no contribution by the defender. Thus we can see the exact apportionment of blame determined by the court. In *Campbell v Gillespie* a mechanic was working at night on a broken down lorry on the A87, between Shiel Bridge and Kyle of Lochalsh. This road is fast in places and it is not lit. The lorry's lights had been disconnected and the mechanic should have provided protection by parking his own, lit vehicle behind the lorry. There was a police warning sign and other vehicles had avoided the lorry before the pursuer's husband ploughed into the back of it at 60mph or faster in his Vauxhall Astra. The car driver was held 60 per cent to blame, the mechanic, 40 per cent.

A further defence is afforded by the doctrine of *volenti non fit injuria* (to one consenting no wrong is done). *Volenti* operates where it can be held that the pursuer has consented to the risk undertaken by the defender. The defender must establish that the pursuer had knowledge of the risk and willingly assented to it. *Volenti* is a complete defence. Where established, it relieves the defender from all liability. The defence of *volenti* does not apply to passengers in road vehicles (Road Traffic Act 1988, s.149). Thus a claim against an over-enthusiastic driver who has crashed cannot be defeated by arguing that the passenger should have asked to leave the vehicle when the dangerous nature of the driving first became apparent. Drivers must by law have third party insurance cover. Where there is no such cover the Motor Insurance Bureau will step in and meet established claims. No such restriction applies to aircraft. In *Morris v Murray* two friends took off in a light aircraft following an afternoon's heavy drinking. The plane crashed shortly after take off and the injured passenger sued the pilot's estate. The defence of *volenti* was successfully established.

It should be noted that *volenti* is not restricted in scope to negligence actions, but is a generally available defence in delict. For example, in the assault case of *Reid v Mitchell* it was argued that the pursuer was *volens* of the risk of falling off the haycart. The defence did not succeed since it was found that the pursuer was not a willing participant in the general larking about.

No liability arises between parties jointly engaged in a criminal undertaking, so if an armed robber is shot by a careless accomplice no civil action arises. The maxim here is *ex turpi causa non oritur actio*. The case of *Weir v Wyper* demonstrates that courts will not allow this defence without regard to the circumstances. A 16-year-old girl allowed herself to be driven home by a young man who held only a provisional driving license. As such she was jointly engaged in an illegal undertaking and the driver sought to rely upon this when she sued him for damages, an accident having occurred on the way home. In the circumstances the pursuer had little option but to act as she did. The journey at the outset had been legal since there had been two other passengers, one of whom held a full driving license. This couple, however, had got out of the car in some remote spot, leaving the pursuer a long way from home with a man she barely knew. The defence was not upheld.

Finally, in exceptional circumstances a defender may plead *damnum fatale*. Broadly, this means "act of God", equivalent to the defence in English law of *vis major*. In *Kerr v Earl of Orkney* the defender sought to attribute the collapse of his dam with consequent property damage to a *damnum fatale*, in this case exceptionally heavy rainfall. The court, however, refused to accept that heavy rainfall in Renfrewshire constituted a *damnum fatale* and it was thought much more likely that the dam had failed from insufficiency of construction since it had survived only four months. To succeed as a defence a *damnum fatale* has to be some unpredictable and overpowering event beyond human control such as a tsunami or volcanic eruption. Indeed, in Scotland seismic activity would seem to be the most likely potential ground for the defence—wet weather in the west cannot be founded upon.

3. LIABILITY FOR NEGLIGENTLY CAUSED ECONOMIC LOSS

INTRODUCTION

At the end of the introductory chapter the student of delict was advised to pay particular attention to the form taken by loss and the form taken by *culpa*. We will see the relevance of this advice again in the following chapter on mental harm, but nowhere, perhaps is the point so important as where the loss suffered is economic; that is, financial.

The issue of *culpa* can be dealt with briefly. Causing economic loss to others is an integral feature of a market economy where competition operates. If a successful company increases its market share by gaining more customers this may be because it has expanded the market. Equally the company may have won customers from less successful competitors. The company may even have driven its competitors out of business quite intentionally. Provided this is not achieved by unlawful means this is *damnum absque injuria*; that is, not a legal wrong. Where unlawful means such as fraud or intimidation are used deliberately to cause financial harm to others then damages may indeed be recovered. In such circumstances the intentional conduct is directed at a victim so no real need to limit the potential scope of liability arises. Intentionally caused economic loss then is reparable so long as it is caused unlawfully.

Unintentionally — that is, negligently caused economic loss — is a different matter. Negligently caused economic loss was unrecoverable until the 1960s. That there could be a duty of care to guard against purely financial harm was first recognised by the House of Lords in *Hedley-Byrne v Heller and Partners*. There have since then been many developments. There was even a brief period near the end of the 1970s, while *Anns v Merton London Borough Council* was the leading authority, when no distinction between economic and other forms of loss was drawn. *Anns* has since been over-ruled in *Murphy v Brentwood District Council*. Duties of care to guard against pure economic loss have now been recognised in many circumstances and criteria established whereby such a duty may be recognised in novel circumstances. There is not, however, a single criteria for determining a duty — there are different approaches which may be taken. The case of *Customs and Excise Commissioners v Barclays Bank* has served to clarify, to an extent, in what circumstances each approach may be taken.

In order to understand what types of economic loss are recoverable it may first be useful to distinguish the different forms such loss may take.

Economic loss can be divided into three forms: derivative, secondary and pure.

Derivative economic loss
Derivative economic losses are those that follow from wrongful invasions of some reparable interest, normally personal injury or death or property damage. Where someone is injured or killed, or their property is damaged in breach of a duty to guard against such harm then there may be financial consequences such as medical expenses, loss of earnings or future earnings, the repair or replacement of property. While clearly economic, such losses are not treated as such by the law. They are not "pure" economic losses. They derive from the invasion of a reparable interest in person or property and form the patrimonial element in an award of damages. Subject to rules on remoteness, derivative economic losses will be recoverable in damages.

Secondary economic loss
There is no liability where a person suffers financial loss consequent on harm caused negligently to somebody else or somebody else's property. This is also known as relational economic loss. The rule serves to limit the number of potential pursuers and to draw a line under the liability of defenders who could otherwise be liable to a degree out of all proportion to the extent of their wrongdoing. Thus, in *Reavis v Clan Line Steamers (No.1)* the pursuer failed to recover losses arising from the death of members of her orchestra when the ship on which they were travelling sank. Her loss arose from her consequent inability to stage performances for which she was contracted. The shipping company, whose negligence was responsible for the deaths, owed duties to the deceased, but owed the pursuer no duty in respect of her losses arising from the inability of the deceased to fulfil their own contracts with her.

So far as property damage is concerned, the leading case in Scots law is *Dynamco v Holland, Hannen & Cubitts*. The pursuers lost production in their factory as the result of a power cut. The defenders had negligently severed a power line. Since the power line was the property of the electricity company and not of the pursuers, the pursuers' losses were secondary and thus not recoverable.

PURE ECONOMIC LOSS

Hedley-Byrne v Heller and Partners
Hedley-Byrne was a firm of advertising agents who had done a small amount of work for a client called Easipower. Easipower had plans for a far more extensive advertising campaign, but because there was some doubt regarding the financial position of Easipower, Hedley-Byrne sought a reference from Easipower's bankers, Heller and Partners via their own bankers, National Provincial. On the strength of the positive reference provided by Heller, Hedley-Byrne went ahead and placed adverts for Easipower. Subsequently Easipower went into liquidation leaving Hedley-

Byrne with losses arising from their performance of the contract of £17,661.18/10d.

The judge at first instance and the Court of Appeal held that no duty of care was owed Hedley-Byrne by Heller. In the House of Lords it was held that a duty of care did arise in the circumstances. However, Hedley-Byrne was unable to recover damages, because the reference had been given with a specific disclaimer of responsibility on the part of Heller.

In *Hedley Byrne* a majority held that a duty of care not to cause economic loss could be recognised in circumstances where there had been an assumption of responsibility on the part of the person making the statement. In addition the pursuer must have relied upon the defender to exercise such a degree of care as the circumstances required. Such reliance must have been reasonable and the defender must have known or ought to have known that the pursuer would rely on the defender's statement.

Hedley Byrne was a landmark decision. This case overruled the earlier decision of the majority of the Court of Appeal in *Candler v Crane Christmas & Co* in which it was held that a contractual or fiduciary relationship between the parties was necessary before a duty of care in negligence could arise. *Hedley Byrne* gave effect to Lord Justice Denning's dissenting opinion in *Candler*.

Hedley Byrne has been applied in a number of subsequent cases in which recovery of damages has been allowed in respect of negligent misstatement. For example, in *Esso Petroleum Co v Mardon* the owners of a petrol station made a careless representation to a prospective tenant regarding the potential throughput of petrol. The tenancy was taken in reliance on this statement. In court it was determined that the owners had held themselves out as having special expertise in circumstances which gave rise to a duty of care.

In *Martin v Bell Ingram* the Inner House held that a surveyor, conducting a house survey under a contract with a building society, owes a duty of care to the prospective buyer of the house, provided that the surveyor knows the survey report will be used and relied upon by that particular buyer. Although surveys are generally instructed by lenders, the prospective purchaser pays for the survey albeit payment is made by the borrower to the lender who in turn pays the surveyor. The House of Lords affirmed this approach in *Smith v Eric S Bush*. In *Smith* the surveyors sought to rely on a disclaimer which excluded liability to anyone other than the building society which had commissioned the report. This disclaimer was subjected to the test of reasonableness under the Unfair Contract Terms Act 1977 and judged to be unreasonable, given that the purchaser had paid for it, albeit indirectly. The important feature of this case is that the existence of the disclaimer was not taken to negative the assumption of responsibility by the defendants; it was relevant only to the issue of whether liability had been validly excluded. There had been a disclaimer sent in *Martin*, but it had arrived too late to have any effect on legal relations between the parties.

Since the coming into force of the Housing (Scotland) Act 2006 sellers now have to make certain materials available to prospective buyers including a "single survey". The Housing (Scotland) Act 2000 (Consequential Provisions) Order 2008 provides for liability in damages to a purchaser suffering loss where the surveyor's report is not based on an inspection of the house, or has not been prepared in a fair and unbiased way, or has not been prepared with reasonable care and skill.

Caparo Industries plc v Dickman

In *Caparo Industries plc v Dickman* the House of Lords held that a negligently prepared company audit could not be used to found a claim when company shareholders successfully mounted a takeover bid on the strength of audited accounts. The accounts showed a profit of £1.3 million whereas the true figure was a loss of £0.46 million. No duty of care was owed the shareholders as potential investors.

In *Hedley Byrne*, and the cases noted above as following it, the party making the statement was aware not only of the identity of the party relying on the statement, but also knew of the particular transaction in respect of which reliance was placed on the statement. In order to satisfy the requirements of proximity, the negligent auditors in *Caparo* would have had to have known that these particular investors would rely on the audit for purposes of their takeover. In *Caparo* the tripartite test outlined in Chapter 2 was laid down. Before a duty could be recognised, loss to the pursuer must be reasonably foreseeable, there had to be a sufficient degree of proximity between the parties and, as a matter of policy it had to be fair, just and reasonable to recognise a duty of care. The recognition of a duty of care in these circumstances would have created potential liability that was far too wide.

Henderson v Merrett Syndicates Ltd

A different test from that developed in *Caparo* was applied in *Henderson v Merrett Syndicates Ltd (No.1)*. Lord Goff took the view that where there was an assumption of responsibility it was not necessary to consider the policy factors in the third part of the *Caparo* test. *Henderson v Merrett* did not involve negligent misstatement, but pure economic loss caused by the negligent provision of services. Under *Henderson* rules, the recognition of a duty of care depends upon a voluntary assumption of responsibility for the economic interests of the pursuer with concomitant reliance on the exercise of the defender's skill and expertise. In other words, the pursuer must rely on the defender's skill and expertise and this reliance must be known to the defender. A disclaimer of responsibility on the part of the defender will prevent a duty from arising since it negates any inference that may be drawn that there has been an assumption of responsibility.

The assumption of responsibility is not imposed on the defender, it may be inferred from the relationship between the parties or from conduct or the terms of any contract between them. This view is confirmed in *Royal Bank of Scotland plc v Bannerman, Johnstone Maclay* in which it was held that the pursuer need not prove that the defender intended to assume responsibility.

It may be noted that a disclaimer of responsibility will serve to prevent a duty from arising in the first place whereas, under *Hedley-Byrne* rules, disclaimers did not have this effect, but could negate liability for negligence once the duty was established. Section 25(5) of the Unfair Contract Terms Act 1977 does, however, apply the reasonableness test to attempts to prevent a duty from arising. The facts in *Bank of Scotland v Fuller Peiser* were as follows. A Mrs Mackay sought a valuation survey on a hotel from a firm of surveyors. The Bank of Scotland, who was lending the money for the purchase, requested the survey directly from the surveyors. The transaction went ahead with the bank taking out a standard security over the hotel. When Mrs Mackay defaulted on the loan the bank sold the hotel and the sale did not realise the full extent of the debt. The survey upon which the bank had relied for valuation of the hotel had been negligently conducted. The bank sought to recover their losses from the surveyors who relied on a disclaimer sent to Mrs MacKay stating that they "accepted no responsibility to any party other than the client".

The disclaimer suggested that the defenders had no intention of assuming responsibility to the bank for the accuracy of the survey. Nonetheless, Lord Eassie held that, in order to be effective, the disclaimer had to pass the reasonableness test under the Unfair Contract Terms Act. Given the circumstances, that the parties were of equal bargaining power and that the bank could well have afforded to instruct an independent survey, the disclaimer was deemed reasonable and so the defenders evaded liability.

In general a solicitor acting for a client acts under a contract and may be concurrently liable to the client in both contract and delict. However, the solicitor owes no duty of care to third parties. There have been moves, however, to recognise the liability of a solicitor to persons who have failed to benefit under a will, because of the solicitor's negligence.

The House of Lords applied the idea of assumption of responsibility in *White v Jones* and ruled by a majority that disappointed beneficiaries could recover in tort in respect of a will that was not drawn up at all. Following a family dispute the deceased had instructed a will that disinherited his daughters. There was a reconciliation and the solicitor was instructed to draft a new will. The solicitor neglected to do this so that, when the testator died, the distribution of the estate was governed by the original will. *White* was followed in Scotland in *Holmes v Bank of Scotland.* There are a number of conceptual difficulties posed by *White*, not least is that it is not clear that beneficiaries would have relied on the defender's skill. Recent Scots cases, *Fraser v McArthur Stewart* and *Matthews v Hunter and Robertson* suggest that the Scots courts are giving *White* a fairly restrictive interpretation.

Caparo or Henderson?

Perhaps unsurprisingly there is some confusion as to the relevant test to be applied for recognition of a duty to guard against pure economic loss. Some guidance is available in the appeal to the House of Lords from *Customs and Excise Commissioners v Barclays Bank.* Faced with a novel case of pure economic loss the first stage is to ask if there is a voluntary assumption of responsibility. If there is, then the existence of a duty can be determined on this basis with no need to invoke policy considerations. If no assumption of responsibility is found this does not end matters. The *Caparo* test should then be applied. The *Caparo* test may give a different result to the assumption of responsibility test since policy considerations may prove decisive.

Defective property
The rules on defective property are, thankfully, clear. If an electrical appliance has some latent defect that causes the buyer's house to burn down, then the cost of rebuilding the house is derivative economic loss and recoverable, since this is an example of defective property damaging other property. Where defective goods cause injury, this is recoverable in principle, although the operative liability regime is now statutory (Consumer Protection Act 1987). The cost of repairing or replacing defective goods that do not harm either other property or persons is only recoverable in contract.

The same principles that apply to defective goods also apply to defective buildings. Thus if a house is built on inadequate foundations, consequent damage to walls in the form of cracking and subsidence is not derivative loss, but there is a defect in the quality of the building which amounts to pure economic loss. This was affirmed by the House of Lords in *Murphy v Brentwood District Council*. Having sought the advice of structural engineers the council had approved plans for a concrete foundation raft to be laid on a landfill site so that two houses could be erected thereon. The engineers had missed flaws in the design, the foundation cracked and subsidence damage occurred to the houses. The owner of one house sold his property for £45,000 less than market value though insurance made up the greater part of his losses. The loss was held to be unrecoverable against the council. A major policy consideration here is that recognition of liability would largely have the effect of shifting the losses between insurers and no good reason was seen for making the local authority's insurer liable as opposed to the homeowner's. Another policy consideration is that the house buyer may have other means of redress, guarantees may be obtained at the time of purchase. Equally, as noted above, where a survey has been relied upon the negligent surveyor may be liable.

A defect that is not dangerous, such as defective plasterwork, does not amount to property damage, but is treated as a defect in quality. As such the financial consequences of defects in buildings are regarded as pure economic loss. There may be a remedy in contract, but in circumstances where the pursuer has no contract with the plasterer, for example, because the defective work was carried out for a builder by a sub-contractor, recovery will not be possible and the loss will lie where it falls (*D&F Estates Ltd v Church Commissioners for England*). There is an exception in Scots law which is discussed below.

Junior Books v The Veitchi Company Ltd

In *Junior Books* a subcontractor was held liable to the owner of premises in respect of the costs of replacing a defective floor. Despite the fact that the subcontractors had no direct contractual relationship with the owners and the loss was pure economic loss since the defective floor was neither dangerous nor likely to cause harm to persons or other property, the House of Lords allowed recovery of damages.

It was significant to the decision that there was a close degree of proximity between the parties. Veitchi, the subcontractor, was nominated by the agent of Junior Books. Thus Veitchi would have known the identity of the owners and that Junior Books would rely on their skill and expertise. Accordingly they would have known that careless performance on their part would result in economic loss to Junior Books.

The essential points about *Junior Books* liability are that the parties should be linked by a series of contracts operating at the same time and the defender must know that the pursuer is relying on the exercise of skill and expertise, from which it follows that the defender must know who the pursuer is. Loss to the pursuer must be reasonably foreseeable to the defender as a consequence of negligently conducted operations.

These circumstances are readily distinguishable from *D&F Estates* since, in that case, the work was complete before the plaintiffs entered into their contract of lease. There was never any link through contracts in place at the same time, nor could the defendants have contemplated loss to these particular plaintiffs.

It may be noted that *Junior Books* dates from the period when *Anns v Merton Borough Council* was in force. English courts have been reluctant to follow it, but it has been applied in a small number of subsequent Scots cases, including: *Scott Lithgow Ltd v GEC Electrical Products Ltd*; *Strathford East Kilbride Ltd v HLM Design Ltd*; and *Comex Houlder Diving Ltd v Colne Fishing Co Ltd (No.2)*. More recently, however, it has been noted by Martin Hogg in *Obligations* that, "*Junior Books* is being frozen out in its own jurisdiction" (2nd edn (Avizandum, 2006), para.3.129). Thus the potential of this case to lay down any principle of general applicability must be severely limited.

---

4. MENTAL HARM

INTRODUCTION

The term "nervous shock" is used in some circumstances as an alternative to psychiatric or mental harm. Medically, the expression may be dubious. However, lawyers tend to persist in the term nervous shock as it indicates the way in which courts have approached this phenomenon. This is true historically, and the idea of an immediate and overwhelming blow to the senses causing mental harm still informs current legal thinking.

While historically courts have been circumspect about the possibility of spurious claims, modern psychiatry is such that there are physical symptoms that may be more easily faked than mental health problems. The law does indeed demand, for a relevant claim, that pursuers suffer some recognised psychiatric condition, such as Post Traumatic Stress Disorder. Following *Simpson v ICI* it is clear that mere anxiety or emotional distress is not sufficient to found a claim.

Finally, it should be noted that there is a growing body of case law involving recovery of damages from employers in respect of psychiatric illness precipitated by stress in the workplace. Currently, the most influential authority in this area is the English Court of Appeal case *Hatton v Sutherland*. Foreseeability of psychiatric harm is a key criterion in recognising a duty of care. This duty has been recognised outwith the employment relationship. In England it has been held that duties of care to avoid causing mental harm can be owed towards those in custody by the police or by prison officers. *Butchart v Home Office* is a recent example of such a case. This is a developing aspect of the law which should perhaps be regarded separately from cases where psychiatric harm follows from a shocking traumatic event. This chapter considers in more detail the latter form of liability for mental harm.

RECOGNITION OF THE PRINCIPLE OF RECOVERY

Initially, courts demonstrated much reluctance in recognising non-physical personal injury as reparable. The policy reason for this attitude is made clear through a number of judicial dicta to the effect that admitting such a form of loss would result in a barrage of spurious claims. At one time, loss in the form of psychiatric harm was simply viewed as too remote. Thus, in 1888, in *Victorian Railway Commissioners v Coultas* the Privy Council refused damages to a lady who had suffered "severe nervous shock" and subsequent illness and miscarriage after a very narrow escape from being run down by a train. However, *Coultas* was not followed two years later in *Bell v Great Northern Railway of Ireland*. The Exchequer Division in Ireland awarded damages to a female train passenger who had suffered nervous shock through fear for her own safety. The railway company was held to be in breach of a duty to convey passengers not only safely, but securely.

In 1891 an award of £500 in damages was given in the Court of Session to a man who suffered nervous shock during a freak rail accident (*Wood v North British Railway Co*). A train coming in the other direction carried a load of pit props that protruded beyond the width of the trucks. When the pursuer's train met the goods train the props broke through the carriage in which the pursuer was a passenger and brought his train to a violent halt. This case went to the House of Lords, but the issue there was whether the pursuer was barred from seeking damages in court having accepted an offer in settlement. The House of Lords did not determine an issue of whether nervous shock was reparable until *Bourhill v Young* in 1943. In *Wood* the award made by the Lord Ordinary was not disturbed. Only the English judges appear to have doubted whether such loss was reparable.

That psychiatric harm is recoverable in principle was only clearly established in English law in *Dulieu v White & Sons*, although there is an earlier example of damages awarded by the Queen's Bench Division in *Wilkinson v Downton*, where the plaintiff was the victim of a joke. This, however, did not involve negligence. In *Dulieu* the Divisional Court of the Kings Bench Division allowed recovery of damages to a woman who had suffered a severe shock when a horse van was negligently driven into the bar in which she worked. The plaintiff was pregnant at the time and later gave premature birth to a child who, as the law report puts it, was "born an idiot". *Dulieu* was subsequently followed in 1908 in the Scottish case of *Wallace v Kennedy*.

Thus, at the beginning of the twentieth century it was clear that psychiatric harm in the form of nervous shock was not too remote to give rise to recovery in damages. Recovery at the time was restricted to those whose shock was caused by fear for their own personal safety rather than fear for the safety of others. Moreover, damages were recoverable even though nervous shock was unaccompanied by physical injury.

REASONABLE FORSEEABILITY

The first case in which damages were recovered where the victim of shock was concerned not for her own safety but for that of her children, was *Hambrook v Stokes Bros* in 1925. This was a majority decision of the Court of Appeal. However, the status of *Hambrook* as an authority remained in doubt following *Bourhill v Young*. *Bourhill* emphasised the importance of reasonable foreseeability of psychiatric harm to the pursuer before a duty of care could arise. As Lord Denning said, 10 years later in *King v Phillips*, "…there can be no doubt since *Bourhill v Young* that the test of liability for shock is foreseeability of injury by shock". In *King* the Court of Appeal denied damages to a mother who had witnessed a taxi driver negligently reversing over her son's tricycle. The plaintiff heard the boy scream from 70 to 80 yards away, but could not see him when the taxi stopped. In fact he was unharmed. Ostensibly, like Mrs Bourhill, the plaintiff was too far from the incident for a duty of care to be owed her. The unacknowledged reason for the decision was one of policy. The court sought to restrict liability for fear of "opening the floodgates" to large number of claims.

In 1967 liability for nervous shock was extended to rescuers. In *Chadwick v British Transport Commission* the plaintiff suffered depression and eventually committed suicide following horrific experiences in aiding victims of the Lewisham train disaster. The view was taken that it was reasonably foreseeable that, in such an event, citizens would come to the rescue and so a duty of care was owed those who did. Moreover, the actions of a rescuer do not constitute a *novus actus interveniens* breaking the chain of causation between the negligent act and resultant harm. This is because the rescuer acts out of moral obligation so their involvement is not treated as voluntary. From a policy point of view it was thought undesirable to deny recovery to selfless and altruistic rescuers.

EXTENSION OF PRINCIPLE OF RECOVERY

In 1983, in *McLoughlin v O'Brian*, the House of Lords allowed recovery in damages to a mother who witnessed the immediate aftermath of a road accident in which her husband and two children were injured and one child was killed. The limiting principle in *Dulieu*, that the shock must result for fear for personal safety, was rejected. The existence of the duty of care owed the plaintiff was based on reasonable foreseeability of psychiatric harm, but the court was also concerned with policy. In order to limit potential claims it was held necessary to have witnessed the incident or its immediate aftermath directly. Mrs McLoughlin arrived at the hospital where her family were held two hours after the accident. In holding that she witnessed the immediate aftermath it was significant that the victims had not been cleaned up, nor had wounds been dressed.

THE CURRENT POSITION

It has been possible to categorise pursuers in terms of participants, bystanders and rescuers, or in terms of those shocked through fear for their own safety as opposed to those shocked through witnessing horrific events befall others. The critical distinction in the modern context is between primary and secondary victims. This follows from the House of Lords cases of *Page v Smith* and *White v Chief Constable of South Yorkshire*. Broadly, a primary victim is a person within the range of potential physical harm. A secondary victim is a person outwith the range of potential physical harm.

Thus, new cases have to be approached, not by identifying the pursuer as a participant, bystander or rescuer, but by enquiring whether the pursuer was within the range of potential physical harm. For example, a rescuer might be either a primary or secondary victim depending upon the circumstances. In *White* the respondent police officers had been involved in assisting victims of the Hillsborough disaster. They were not held entitled to damages as they had not been in physical danger themselves. They were not, therefore, primary victims and moreover were unable to satisfy the requirements for recovery of damages demanded of secondary victims. By contrast in *Hale v London Underground* a fireman successfully recovered damages for nervous shock. He had assisted in the Kings Cross disaster while the incident was still occurring. He had been exposed to considerable danger. Subsequently he suffered horrendous nightmares and severe depression. On his return to work he was only able to do a desk job.

A note of caution may be added. The way in which the distinction is drawn between primary and secondary victims is not entirely settled. Recent decisions in Scottish courts, noted at the end of this chapter, have cast some doubt upon whether the criteria for being a primary victim is truly settled as having been within the range of foreseeable harm.

PRIMARY VICTIMS

In *Page v Smith* a man suffered a re-occurrence of Myalgic Encephalomyelitis (ME) when the stationary car in which he was sitting was bumped by the defendant's car. ME was regarded by the court at the time as a form of mental harm. Research suggests that its provenance as a medical condition is in some doubt. Clearly drivers owe a duty of care to other drivers and pedestrians within the range of potential harm not to cause personal injury or damage their property. However, it was arguable that while physical harm might have been reasonably foreseeable, psychiatric harm was not. Nevertheless, damages were awarded.

It follows from *Page* that where a duty of care not to cause physical injury is established and psychiatric harm results from the defender's negligence, the defender will be liable. In the case of primary victims psychiatric harm need not be reasonably foreseeable. Of course physical harm must be reasonably foreseeable or there would be no duty, but physical harm need not materialise for a claim to be valid. Effectively, where primary victims are concerned, the concept of personal injury has been broadened to include psychiatric harm.

In order to claim as a primary victim the pursuer must be exposed to danger or must reasonably apprehend themselves to be in danger.

In *Rothwell v Chemical and Insulating Co Ltd* one of the appellants had received a diagnosis of pleural plaques. This condition is asymptomatic, it does not affect physical health and does not lead to any illness. The presence of pleural plaques however, is indicative of exposure to asbestos and the appellant had sought damages against the employer who had negligently exposed him to asbestos some thirty years earlier. Knowledge of this exposure had caused anxiety about developing a serious illness to the point that the appellant suffered clinical depression. It may be noted that this was not a case of a reaction to some immediate traumatic event. The House of Lords refused to extend the application of *Page* to cover these circumstances. It was held that pleural plaques did not constitute loss, the appellant was actually seeking damages for psychiatric harm caused by apprehending the possibility of something which had not taken place.

SECONDARY VICTIMS

Secondary victims have not been exposed to physical danger themselves. Nevertheless, they have suffered nervous shock, typically as a consequence of witnessing horrific events that have befallen primary victims, such as relatives or colleagues. The circumstances in which secondary victims may recover damages in respect of nervous shock are strictly limited and courts take a highly restrictive approach in such cases. In contrast to primary victims, no duty of care to guard against psychiatric harm will arise unless such harm is a reasonably foreseeable consequence of breach.

Reasonable foreseeability of psychiatric harm is a necessary, but not sufficient condition for the existence of a duty of care. In addition, secondary victims have to satisfy three further "proximity" requirements that were established by the House of Lords in the Hillsborough disaster case brought by relatives of the primary victims, *Alcock v Chief Constable of South Yorkshire*. No duty will arise unless: a tie of love and affection is established between the secondary and primary victim; the secondary victim is present at the event or its immediate aftermath; and perception of the event or its immediate aftermath must be direct. Direct perception means that the secondary victim must personally see or hear the event. If the pursuer is told of the incident by a third party the claim will not be met.

The tie of love and affection between primary and secondary victims may be readily presumed in some relationships, for example, between husband and wife or parent and child. However, other relationships are not precluded so in theory recovery should be possible where the primary victim is the same sex partner of the secondary victim or the parties are very close, but not united by any conventional category of relationship. The critical factor is not the type of relationship, but its strength and this is a matter upon which evidence may have to be led. In *Alcock* the first appellant, Robert Alcock, lost his brother in law. Another appellant, Brian Harrison, lost two brothers. Neither was able to recover in respect of nervous shock in the absence of evidence to show that their relationships with the deceased were particularly close.

Of those appellants whose ties with the primary victims could be presumed, their cases failed because they could not satisfy either or both the other two proximity requirements. Some of the appellants did not arrive at the scene until some eight hours after the event and this was held to be too remote in time to count as presence at the aftermath. The direct perception requirement was not satisfied in some cases where the appellants had learned of the tragedy on television or heard about it on the radio.

THE STATE OF THE LAW

The view was expressed in *Alcock* that it would not be in every case that all three proximity requirements would require to be satisfied. However, subsequent cases, such as *Robertson v Forth Road Bridge Joint Board (No.2)*, in which the pursuer watched his workmate and drinking buddy of 20 years fall to his death, and *McFarlane v EE Caledonia Ltd*, in which an oil worker on a supply vessel witnessed at close proximity the series of explosions on the Piper Alpha oil platform, demonstrate the highly restrictive approach taken by the courts where secondary victims are concerned. In neither case did the pursuer succeed. The pursuers were not held to have been involved in the events in a way that would have allowed recovery as primary victims. Their ties with the primary victims were not such as to allow recovery as secondary victims. More recently in *Keen v Tayside Contracts* the pursuer was asked by his supervisor to assist at a particularly gruesome road accident and was refused permission to leave. He was unable to recover in respect of consequent mental harm since he was classed as a secondary victim and had no ties to the victims.

In *Taylorson v Shieldness Produce Ltd* recovery was denied parents who suffered psychiatric illness when their child took three days to die, thus demonstrating the persistence of the idea that reparable mental harm must follow some sudden, shocking event. On the same basis, in *Sion v Hampstead Health Authority* a father who suffered mental illness having maintained a two-week vigil at the bedside of his dying son was also unable to recover damages. These cases may be contrasted with *Tredget v Bexley Health Authority* in which the birth and, two days later, death of a child born with serious injuries was treated effectively as a single event.

In *Young v Charles Church (Southern) Ltd* the plaintiff was a scaffolder. When his back was turned a workmate shorted out an overhead power cable with a scaffolding pole. The plaintiff was held by the Court of Appeal to have been within the area of physical danger and recovered damages as a primary victim. However, the point has been made that his nervous shock appears to have been attributable more to witnessing the horrific accident that befell his mate rather than out of fear for personal safety. Considered in the light of *Robertson*, *McFarlane* and the subsequent case of *Hunter v British Coal*, Mr Young appears to have been treated by the courts with uncharacteristic generosity.

In the Scottish case of *Campbell v North Lanarkshire County Council* the pursuer witnessed the horrific aftermath of a series of electrical explosions. The nature of their injuries rendered the appearance of the victims, with whom the pursuer had been working, particularly ghastly. The pursuer returned to the site of the explosion to assist the victims. The pleadings in court focussed upon whether or not the pursuer was a primary victim. Although he had left the scene shortly before the accident, when he returned the event was still continuing. On the basis of his pleadings he appears to have had reasonable grounds to believe himself in danger. Lord Reed allowed a proof before answer, taking the view that the case could not be determined upon pleadings alone. Before reaching a decision, it was held necessary to hear evidence on both sides regarding the risks to which the pursuer was exposed.

Two recent decisions in Scottish cases serve to confuse the way in which the distinction between primary and secondary victims is to be drawn. In *Salter v UB Frozen and Chilled Foods Ltd* the pursuer, who was involved in an incident in which a fellow employee was killed, was held to be a primary victim even though he was in no danger himself and was in no way to blame for the death. The temporary sheriff in this case founded his ruling on the criteria for primary victims laid down by Lord Oliver in *Alcock* rather than on *Page v Smith*. Lord Oliver had defined primary victims as being "directly involved in the accident". In *Anderson v Christian Salvesen plc* the pursuer was a lorry driver who had inadvertently killed a fellow employee by reversing his lorry while the victim was loading the trailer on a fork lift truck. Again, the lorry driver was not at fault. In this Outer House case Lord Drummond Young accorded the pursuer the status of a primary victim on grounds that he was instrumental in the victim's death.

It is probably fair to say that the current state of the law is regarded as satisfactory by nobody. In England in 1998 the Law Commission argued for reform (Law Com. No.249). In 2004 The Scottish Law Commission called for radical reform (Scot. Law Com. No.196). The draft Reparation for Mental Harm (Scotland) Bill appended to the report provides inter alia for the abolition of common law rules applying only to mental harm. It is proposed to wipe the slate clean and put liability for mental harm on a statutory basis.

---

5. VICARIOUS LIABILITY

INTRODUCTION

Vicarious liability concerns the liability of one party for the delictual acts or omissions of another. It can be explained as a modification to the general rule, *culpa tenet suos auctores* (fault binds its authors). Two other maxims are commonly used to justify this modification, *qui facit per alium facit per se* (where one does a thing through the instrumentality of another, he is held as having done it himself) and *respondeat superior* (let the master answer).

In short, while it is normally the case that parties will only be liable for their own conduct, vicarious liability may arise where a delict is committed by a person acting on another's behalf. Where a servant (employee) commits a delict the master (employer) can be called upon to answer for it.

Vicarious liability operates in employment, in agency and in partnership. In all these situations there are relationships in which one party acts on behalf of another. So the employer may be vicariously liable for the acts of employees, the principal for the acts of agents and the other partners for the acts of a single partner. Most of the case law concerns the employer/employee relationship, but similar considerations apply to the other relationships. In agency, for example, the criterion for vicarious liability is whether the agent has acted within the scope of their authority. On vicarious liability for acts of an agent, see, for example, *Launchbury v Morgans*. On the vicarious liability of partners see *Dubai Aluminium Co Ltd v Salaam*.

It has been argued that vicarious liability is not so much a matter of legal principle as policy. Where an employer conducts an enterprise that creates risks for others, it is fair that the employer should pay for the consequences of the risks when they materialise. The employer does, after all, take the benefits of the enterprise. The fact that the enterprise is conducted through the instrumentality of others (employees do the work) does not absolve the employer from meeting whatever liabilities arise from the conduct of the enterprise. Moreover, vicarious liability operates as a prompt to employers to promote safe conduct and practices in carrying out the enterprise.

The practical effect of vicarious liability is to give the victim a defender worth suing. Imagine you suffer extensive injuries caused by the negligent driving of a fork lift truck in your local do-it-yourself store. The delinquent truck driver is on a relatively low wage and has no financial assets to speak of. He could not hope to compensate you for your losses. On the other hand the employer, a corporation with substantial assets and a turnover of many millions, is in a position easily to meet your claims. Moreover, the employer will probably have insurance that covers such losses. Where the victim is an employee, insurance is compulsory under the Employer's Liability (Compulsory Insurance) Act 1969.

It is important to note that vicarious liability arises not only from negligence, but also from intentional wrongdoing. For example, in *Morris v CW Martin & Sons Ltd* an employee committed the tort of conversion by stealing a mink stole deposited with the defendants for cleaning. The employers were vicariously liable to the plaintiff for her loss. In *Photo Production Ltd v Securicor Transport Ltd* an employee deliberately started a fire that burned down the factory he was supposed to be guarding. It was held that vicarious liability arose. Vicarious liability may also arise in respect of fraud. *Taylor v Glasgow District Council* demonstrates that in order for vicarious liability to arise it is not necessary to show that the employer gained any benefit thereby.

Where one party is held vicariously liable, the delinquent is not released from liability. Vicarious liability is imposed in addition to the liability of the party at fault. Liability is joint and several. The pursuer may elect to sue either or both parties. In theory the vicariously liable party may recover damages paid to the pursuer from the party at fault as occurred in *Lister v Romford Ice*. In practice this seldom happens.

It should be noted that even where vicarious liability is not established, a case against the defender may be maintained if it can be established that the defender was personally liable to the pursuer. It is not unusual to see a plea of vicarious liability advanced as an alternative to an averment of personal liability. An example would be where a person is injured on trade premises by a falling slate dropped by an employee who is fixing the roof. The employer might be vicariously liable for the negligence of the employee, but could also be personally liable as occupier for harm done due to the state of the building under the Occupiers' Liability (Scotland) Act 1960.

It is not in every case that employers will be held vicariously liable. If you step on a landmine, laid as an illegal remedy against dog fouling in my front garden, there will be no point in seeking reparation from my employer. The delict in this example bears no relation to my employment. Of course there are many situations where the issue of vicarious liability is not so clear cut as in this example. For vicarious liability to arise, the delict must be sufficiently connected to the delinquent's employment. The basic features involved in determining whether conduct gives rise to vicarious liability will be considered below.

The other difficulty found in vicarious liability is in determining for whom the employer is liable. In general, employers are vicariously liable for employees, i.e. those under a contract of service *locatio operarum* and not for independent contractors, those under a contract for services *locatio operis faciendi*. However, allocating particular relationships to either category is not always as straightforward as might be thought. This distinction is also considered below.

EMPLOYEE ACTING WITHIN THE SCOPE OF EMPLOYMENT

A good starting point for a Scots text is a dictum of Lord President Clyde in *Kirby v NCB*. An English text would start with *Salmond on Torts*, the source from which Lord Clyde derived his formulation:

> "In the decisions four different types of situation have been envisaged as guides to the solution of this problem. [1] In the first place, if the master actually authorised the particular act, he is clearly liable for it. [2] Secondly, where the workman does some work which he is appointed to do, but does it in a way which his master has not authorised and would not have authorised had he known of it, the master is nevertheless still responsible for the servant's act is still within the scope of his employment. [3] On the other hand in the third place, if the servant is employed only to do a particular work or a particular class of work, and he does something outside the scope of that work, the master is not responsible for any mischief the servant may do to a third party. [4] Lastly, if the servant uses his master's time or his master's tools for his own purposes, the master is not responsible."

Categories [1] and [4] are relatively clear. The difficulties that arise in practice concern the distinction between [2] and [3]. An unauthorised mode of doing an authorised act [2] gives rise to vicarious liability, but an act that is outwith the scope of employment, i.e. completely independent of the employer's business [3] does not. However, independent acts may give rise to vicarious liability if they are sufficiently connected with the employer's business. This is considered further below under "recent developments".

In *Kirby* the pursuer was a mine employee who had gone to a part of the pit away from his working place for a smoke. The defender, the employer, was not liable for the injuries sustained in an explosion when a match was lit by an unidentified miner. Going for a smoke was not in any way connected with the pursuer's work, it was done purely for his own purposes and pleasure and, incidentally, was in breach of statute. The pursuer had acted outwith the scope of his employment.

Still on the subject of smoking, the difference between [2] and [3] may be illustrated by contrasting *Kirby* with *Century Insurance Co Ltd v Northern Ireland Road Transport Board*. In an act of monumental stupidity the driver of a fuel tanker lit a cigarette and discarded a match while draining 300 gallons of petrol from his tanker into a garage storage tank. The resulting explosion damaged the garage owner's car and several houses. In this case the driver was acting within the scope of his employment and his employers were therefore vicariously liable. Lighting the cigarette was an unauthorised act, but done while the driver was doing his job. As Lord Chancellor Viscount Simon quoted, "[t]hey also serve who stand and wait". It was the driver's duty to watch over the delivery. He was negligent in the discharge of his duty, but he was actively discharging his duty while negligent, therefore he was acting within the scope of his employment. *Century Insurance* falls within [2].

The reason *Kirby* was unsuccessful in his claim was that he was "off on a frolic of his own", rather than acting within the scope of his employment. Similarly, in *McLean v Remploy Ltd* the pursuer was the victim of a practical joke, played on him by other, unidentified employees who had tied a length of yarn across a corridor. The Lord Ordinary (Cameron) held that employers could not be held vicariously liable for such frolics. However, such cases turn on their own circumstances and in *Harrison v Michelin Tyre Co Ltd* the defender was found vicariously liable when an employee was injured by a prank. The critical feature has been whether or not the act can be deemed to be within the scope of employment.

The courts have demonstrated a clear tendency to find vicarious liability so long as the employer's purposes are being pursued when the delict is committed. This is so even though the employer's rules have been broken. In *Rose v Plenty* a milkman hired a 13-year-old boy to assist with deliveries in flagrant breach of dairy policy. The boy was injured when the milkman drove the float negligently. The dairy was found vicariously liable since the boy's presence on the float was in pursuance of the employer's business.

The following three examples concern drivers who deviated from their most direct routes in the course of carrying out their employers' instructions. In all these cases employers were found vicariously liable on the basis that the delinquent employees were conducting authorised work in an unauthorised way. Each case demonstrates in successive fashion the extent to which courts will go in order to hold that acts are within the scope of employment and therefore employers are liable. In *Angus v Glasgow Corporation* a lorry driver took a short deviation from his route in order to collect his spectacles from home. He collided with a car. The car driver sued the lorry driver's employers in negligence. In *RJ McLeod v South of Scotland Electricity Board* a van struck and damaged a footbridge that the pursuers were constructing. The driver had been authorised to take the vehicle home, but when a few hundred yards from home he had gone out of his way to drop off a fellow employee and had then taken a further diversion to visit his mother-in-law. The Lord Ordinary (Wylie) held that the original authorised purpose of the journey had not been wholly superseded.

The final case, *Williams v Hemphill*, which went all the way to the House of Lords, shows the most outrageous deviation. A driver was employed to take a boys' brigade company from Benderloch in Knapdale home to Glasgow. Some of the boys prevailed upon the driver to go to Dollar in Clackmannanshire. This was in order to see once again a party of girl guides whom the boys had helped with luggage at Connel station.

Instead of turning down the A82 at Crianlarich which would have taken them down Loch Lomondside and into Glasgow by Dumbarton, the driver headed by the A85 and A84 for Stirling from where he took an eccentric route for Dollar by the south bank of the Forth and Kincardine. This deviation took the party directly away from Glasgow. Through negligent driving the lorry was overturned on a corner heading into Dollar and there were injuries and fatalities. At all stages of the litigation it was held that the employer was vicariously liable. The dominant purpose of the journey was transportation of the boys to Glasgow, the driver was still engaged in this purpose and the deviation by Dollar was not an independent journey.

RECENT DEVELOPMENTS

The three driver cases and *Rose v Plenty* demonstrate that a broad view is taken of whether conduct is within the scope of employment. Nevertheless, problems have emerged with the old approach that seeks to distinguish between unauthorised modes of doing work and independent acts. A new approach to determining vicarious liability has been pioneered in the Canadian Supreme Court and accepted and applied by the House of Lords in the English case of *Lister v Hesley Hall Ltd*. The new approach is very much a development on the old rather than a departure.

The House of Lords in *Lister* approached vicarious liability as a matter of policy rather than principle and considered that the issue really was whether, in the circumstances, it would be fair and just to impose on the employer liability for the conduct complained of. On the *Lister* model the question whether circumstances give rise to vicarious liability will depend on the outcome of the close connection test. Under this test it must be determined whether an act is *sufficiently connected* to employment for it to be fair and just to hold the employer vicariously liable.

The application of this test can be explored through the case law in which the new approach was developed. Courts will consider the strength of the connection with employment and will seek to differentiate cases where employment has merely provided an opportunity for the acts complained of. In *Bazley v Curry* an employee in a residential care home sexually abused one of the children in his care. The acts were sufficiently connected with his employment for the employers to be held vicariously liable. By contrast, in *Jacobi v Griffiths* an employee at a children's recreational club sexually abused a brother and sister who attended the club. With the exception of one incident, the abuse took place at the defendant's home. The fact that the defendant had met the children at the club did not establish a sufficiently close connection between the acts and employment. The employers were held by a majority of the Canadian Supreme Court not to be vicariously liable. In *Lister v Hesley Hall Ltd* the warden of a school boarding house sexually abused children in his care in a systematic fashion. There was sufficient connection between the acts and employment for the employers to be held vicariously liable.

The logic of these decisions is clear, but the results are not necessarily those that would be reached under the old approach. This may be demonstrated by reference to *Trotman v North Yorkshire County Council*. The deputy headmaster of a special school was charged with responsibility for caring for a disabled teenager on a foreign holiday. The teacher sexually abused the boy. In seeking to distinguish between unauthorised modes of work and independent acts the Court of Appeal found the employers were not vicariously liable. This was not a wrong decision in a legal sense, though it produced an unjust result. Far from being an unauthorised mode of carrying out a duty, the acts were held to be a negation of the duty and thus independent. *Trotman* was overruled by the House of Lords in *Lister*.

Lister has since been applied in Scotland, for example in *M v Hendron*, in which the court accepted in principle that employers could be vicariously liable in respect of the sexual abuse of a boy by monks staffing an approved residential school. It appears from English cases that *Lister* has had the effect of broadening the scope of vicarious liability. A slightly different approach, however, appears to be developing in Scotland. Rather than abandoning the traditional question whether the acts were carried out in the course of employment, this test may still be applied in the process of considering whether there is a close connection. This retains the traditional approach within the new test. This approach may be seen in Inner House case of *Wilson v Exel UK Ltd*.

FOR WHOM IS THE EMPLOYER LIABLE?

Vicarious liability is dependent upon the relationship between the delinquent and the liable party. Employers are liable for the delicts of employees, but not for those of independent contractors. In many instances the distinction between employees and contractors is easily made. In employment the parties are linked by a contract of employment which is either permanent or for a fixed term. The contract terminates at the expiry of the term or following the period of notice according to the contract terms. Equally, the employee may be dismissed. This is a contract of service (*locatio operarum*). A contractor on the other hand is on a contract to perform some specific task or service. The contract terminates when the obligations have been discharged, normally when the work has been completed or the service rendered and payment has been made. This is a contract for services (*locatio operis faciendi*).

The difference may be illustrated by comparing a taxi driver, whom one employs in order to get from A to B on a one-off basis, with a chauffeur, employed to drive one's Bentley wherever and whenever one wishes to go. The former is a contractor, the latter is an employee.

Problems arise where the nature of the contract between the delinquent and the employer is unclear or ambiguous. One test that has been used to determine the distinction between employees and contractors concerns the element of control. According to the control test, where the employer can tell the other party not only what to do but also how to do it, the relationship is one of employment. While this approach works well in respect of unskilled work, it is less useful where work is skilled or specialised. For example, when the server is down in the Law School it is the job of the network supervisor to get it running again, but neither the Dean nor the Principal himself can tell the supervisor how to do it. Nevertheless, the supervisor is an employee.

There is a wide range of factors that can be taken into account in determining the nature of the relationship. The element of control may be a factor depending on circumstances. Other factors include: the extent to which the person is integrated into the organisation as a whole; whether the party runs a commercial risk; the intention of the parties; whether payment is in the form of regular wages or salary or for "the job"; whether employers' national insurance contributions are made; whether tax is deducted as PAYE or the party makes their own tax arrangements; pension arrangements; and the way in which the contract may be terminated.

By taking into account multiple factors according to the circumstances, rather than adhering to a rigid test, the courts are able to produce just results in a multiplicity of differing contractual arrangements. So, for example, in *Short v J&W Henderson Ltd* a docker was held to be an employee of the defending company despite working arrangements very different from that which we would naturally think of as employment.

The defenders were responsible for shipping and unloading a cargo of cement at Campeltown harbour. Dockers at Campeltown were organised so that, whenever a ship was due in, a sufficient number of dockers to unload the cargo was allocated on a strict rota basis. The allocation was made by the local trade union secretary, himself a docker, who took part on the rota in turn. There was no foreman or any docker in charge. The shippers paid a lump sum for the discharge of the cargo to a broker, who in turn paid that sum to whichever docker had been sent to receive payment. The dockers involved on each occasion then divided the money equally between themselves. The broker stamped the National Health and Unemployment Insurance card of any docker employed for the first time that week, seeking the employers' contribution from the shippers. When three dockers were injured in an accident, it was held in the House of Lords that each docker was under an individual contract of employment with the shipper. A number of factors were deemed relevant and the requirement of control was held satisfied by the fact that the brokers, as agents of the employers, had regularly attended the unloading. This pointed to supervision. While there had never been any need to dismiss or suspend a docker, it was found that had such a need occurred this power would have been exercised by the broker on the shipper's behalf.

In one further example, *United Wholesale Grocers Ltd v Sher*, warehouse owners contracted with the defender for joinery work. Sher entrusted the job to three workmen who were paid daily without any deductions for tax or national insurance. Allegedly, one of the workmen negligently discarded a cigarette that caused a fire in the warehouse. The pursuers sought to hold Sher vicariously liable. In the Outer House Lord Cullen had to determine whether the workmen were employees or independent contractors. While the control exercised by Sher over the way in which the work was done was an important factor, it was not conclusive. This was particularly so since supervision of the men was not necessary in the circumstances. The status of the workmen depended on assessment of all relevant factors. Sher supplied the materials, but the workmen supplied their own tools. It fell to be considered whether the work carried out should be regarded as part and parcel of a business carried out by Sher, or as part of what the men were doing on their own account. Lord Cullen came to the conclusion that they were employees of Sher carrying out work on the warehouse that Sher had contracted to undertake.

In general, employers cannot be held vicariously liable for the delicts of independent contractors, although they may become personally liable to their own employees if an incompetent contractor is appointed in breach of the employer's duty to take reasonable care for the safety of employees. Equally, a party who owes a duty, such as an obligation of support under the law of the tenement, cannot avoid liability by appointing an independent contractor to carry out hazardous work. The most recent example of such a case is *Stewart v Malik*.

There is one exceptional case, *Marshall v William Sharp & Sons Ltd*, in which an employee's widow was able to recover from his employer for the delict of an independent contractor, despite a finding that there was no element of personal liability. The pursuer's husband was a quarry manager who died while checking an electrode spark in a burner. The contractor was an electrician who fired both ignition and fuel buttons on the burner when testing it. The electrician was the only one employed at the quarry and he was perpetually available to the quarry. Working at the quarry took up most of his time. Nevertheless, the Inner House determined that the electrician was an independent contractor, but the defenders were vicariously liable for his act. This case is regarded as controversial, although it has been argued that the decision can be supported on grounds of the degree of control exercised by the defenders over the electrician.

PRO HAC VICE EMPLOYMENT

Finally, the situation sometimes arises when courts have to determine which of two different employers is vicariously liable for the delict of an employee. This arises where an employee is lent out or hired. In general, liability rests with the employer with whom the employee has a contract of employment. However, if *pro hace vice* employment is established this means that the borrower may become vicariously liable. The employer who borrows the person will only become vicariously liable if it can be established that full control over not only what the employee does, but how the employee does it, has passed to the borrowing employer. *Sime v Sutcliffe Catering (Scotland) Ltd* is an example where *pro hac vice* employment was established. The pursuer's employers were vicariously liable to her in respect of the negligence of outside caterers contracted to operate in her place of work.

Pro hac vice employment is not determined by any contractual agreement between the two employers. Thus, even though a contract provides that the party is to be regarded as a servant of the borrowing employer, this cannot be relied upon in an issue with a third party who was not a party to the contract. In the House of Lords case of *Mersey Docks and Harbour Board v Coggins & Griffith (Liverpool) Ltd* the defendants, a firm of stevedores, borrowed a crane and driver from the Harbour Board. It was held that while the stevedores told the crane driver what to do, the way in which he did it was a matter within his own discretion. This discretion had been delegated to him by the Harbour Board. When the crane driver negligently injured an employee of Coggins & Griffith, the Harbour Board was held vicariously liable.

6. DEFAMATION

INTRODUCTION

There is a legally protected interest in what Stair described as "fame, reputation and honour" (Stair, I, 4, 4). People are entitled to conduct their daily lives without having their characters besmirched or their reputation dragged through the mud by the dissemination of untrue communications. A person's interest in their reputation is a reparable interest. Accordingly, where that interest is harmed, damages may be sought. Equally, interdict may be sought in order to prevent an injurious publication or broadcast from taking place.

The interest in honour and reputation is protected primarily by the law of defamation, but there are other doctrines that may be appropriate according to the circumstances. There may be a remedy under verbal injury where a person is harmed by false words that are not defamatory. The right to publish true facts about people or publish photographs of them may be limited by the law on breach of confidence. In *Spring v Guardian Royal Exchange* the pursuer was unable to find work in the insurance industry after a reference containing false and defamatory statements was written for him by his previous employers. He sued successfully in negligence. The House of Lords treated this as a case of economic loss in which the plaintiff had relied upon the defendants to state facts accurately. It was held by a majority of four to one that there was sufficient proximity between the parties for a duty to arise and there were no policy reasons to deny recovery in damages.

Had the action been raised in defamation the defence of qualified privilege would have applied. The plaintiff would have been required to prove malice on the part of the defendants and this he could not do. Thus the law of negligence allowed recovery of damages in circumstances where recovery would have been denied under the law of defamation.

ESTABLISHING DEFAMATION

There are three fundamental elements of defamation. The statement must be defamatory, it must be false and there must be malice. It has been said that there must be loss, but personal affront is sufficient to amount to loss, there need be no patrimonial or economic loss. The only further requirement is that the statement must have been communicated. In England, to be actionable, a statement must be communicated to a third party. In Scotland the requirement for communication can be satisfied by communication to the pursuer (*Ramsay v Maclay*). The Scots approach to the rule on communication reflects the availability of solatium for affront or injury to feelings and the fact that there need be no patrimonial loss.

Defamatory capacity

The focus of the pursuer's effort is likely to be on establishing the defamatory capacity of the statement complained of and the fact that they have been defamed. Whether a statement has the capacity to defame is a question of law. Whether the statement has actually defamed the pursuer is a question of fact.

Whether words are defamatory may be determined by the application of a test laid down by Lord Atkin in *Sim v Stretch*: "[w]ould the words tend to lower the plaintiff in the estimation of right-thinking members of society generally?"

The test is thus objective. The issue is not what the pursuer understands the words to mean, neither is it relevant to consider what the defender meant by the words. Whether a statement is defamatory is determined by the views of "right-thinking" people. Of course, the court determines what "right-thinking" people think. "Right-thinking" people are reasonable persons who do not hold prejudices.

This brings us to innuendo. Innuendo is the way in which a meaning may be attributed to words that is not present on the face of the statement. For example, the statement that X is a thief is prima facie defamatory. The statement that X holds a surprising quantity of electrical goods in a lock up garage is not. However, depending on the circumstances in which the statement is made, it may bear the innuendo that either X is a thief or X deals in stolen goods. The onus lies on the pursuer to establish that the statement complained of bears the innuendo contended for.

As Lord Anderson put it in *Duncan v Associated Scottish Newspapers Ltd*, the question that must be asked is:

"[W]ould a reasonable man, reading the publication complained of, discover in it matter defamatory of the pursuer? Or, put otherwise, the question is, What meaning would the ordinary reader of the newspaper put upon the paragraph which the pursuer complained of?"

There is also a subjective element in the test for defamation. In determining defamatory capacity, courts must take into account the type of person likely to have heard or read the statement, the personal circumstances of the pursuer and all the circumstances in which the statement is made. For example, a statement about a rugby player printed in a match programme, that X is "a hard-drinking brute with an expansive repertoire of obscene verse who handles balls better than Gavin Hastings" might be both intended and regarded as complimentary. The same statement, applied to a choirmaster and published in the Church of Scotland periodical, *Life & Work*, would be defamatory. The point is that what may be deeply injurious in one context can be unobjectionable in another. The law takes context into account.

Malice

While liability in defamation is based on malice, the pursuer is not required to prove malice on the part of the defender. Once the statement complained of is established as defamatory, malice is presumed from the harmful nature of the words used. Malice is the natural inference to be drawn. There are, however, circumstances in which this inference may be displaced by a more likely explanation; so, where the defence of fair retort applies the natural inference is that the defender was motivated by the desire to clear his or her own name; where the defence of qualified privilege applies the natural inference is that the defender was motivated by a sense of duty. Both of these defences, where established, have the effect of casting on the pursuer the burden of proving malice. Malice may be established by proof either of *animus injuriandi* that is, intent to harm or proof that the defender made his or her communication without believing it to be true, malice being the natural inference to be drawn from spreading lies about people.

Falsity

Defamatory statements are false statements. It is not for the pursuer to prove that the communication is untrue, falsity, like malice, is presumed from the defamatory nature of the statement. The defender may lead the defence of *veritas* meaning truth, but the onus falls on the defender to prove this. Since a defamatory statement is by definition false *veritas*, where established, is a complete defence. In English law this defence is known as justification.

Innocent defamation

The presumption of malice in defamation is one aspect of the law that might be thought to be unsatisfactory. It offends against the general idea of no liability without fault since liability may be incurred without there ever having been any intent to harm. The classic example of innocent defamation is the case of *Hulton v Jones*, in which the author of a novel created a fictional character with the unlikely name of Artemus Jones. This Artemus Jones was a churchwarden from Peckham who absconded to France with a lady who was not his wife. Unfortunately for the author there was a real Artemus Jones. Doubly unfortunate was the fact that Artemus Jones was a barrister. The defendant was liable in £1,750 damages, a substantial sum at the time, since the plaintiff convinced the House of Lords that readers would understand the story as referring to him. The innocence of this defamation may be open to question since the real Artemus Jones had been employed previously as a sub-editor at the *Sunday Chronicle*, the newspaper which published the story.

The possibility of innocent defamation is real since liability attaches not only to the person making the defamatory statement, but also to those who repeat or disseminate it. This obviously extends to newspaper editors and to broadcasters, but also includes bookshops, libraries and the operators of web pages. The ability of such persons to verify facts or check for defamatory content may be very limited. There is, however, a defence under s.1 of the Defamation Act 1996 that one is not the author, editor or publisher of the statement.

TYPES OF DEFAMATORY STATEMENT

There is no fixed list of possible defamations. The beauty of Lord Atkin's formulation for determining whether a statement is defamatory is its flexibility. It allows for changing perceptions, what will tend to lower a person in the estimation of reasonable people changes over time. This is particularly true when there is a moral dimension to the communication. It is less likely that the courts would now award damages in respect of allegations of: a lack of womanly delicacy (*Cuthbert v Linklater*); sex before marriage (*Morrison v Ritchie*); or an accusation that a person is a blackguard (*Brownlie v Thomson*). In the past imputations of insanity, or "loathsome disease", or male impotence were actionable as defamation but it seems unlikely that these would be actionable now. On the other hand, an allegation that a person suffers from a sexually transmitted disease might be innuendoed as an allegation of sexual profligacy which might indeed be defamatory.

While in *Liberace v Daily Mirror* damages were awarded when a published statement carried an innuendo of homosexuality, *Quilty v Windsor* establishes that such an allegation is no longer defamatory. By the same token, allegations that would not in the past have been defamatory might be so now. Examples might be allegations of beating your children or of drinking and driving. Other examples are a little more difficult to gauge. In 1908 in *Finburgh v Moss Empires Ltd* the manager of a theatre asked a married couple to leave, calling the wife a "notorious prostitute". The wife succeeded in recovering damages, as she would now; the husband did not. Might the suggestion that a man kept company with a prostitute be considered defamatory in the present?

False imputations of criminal conduct have proven a fertile source of litigation. Nevertheless, it is not every imputation of criminal conduct that will give rise to liability in defamation since the test of lowering the pursuer in the estimation of "right-thinking" people must be satisfied. All crimes do not carry the same level of social stigma. Accusations or imputations of murder (*Monson v Tussauds*), theft (*Neville v C&A Modes*), lewd and libidinous practices or shameless indecency will clearly have the effect of reducing the social esteem in which a person is held. In *Gecas v Scottish Television* an action was brought by a party accused of involvement in the liquidation of Jews during the Second World War. Such an accusation is defamatory, but this case was successfully defended since the allegations were true. There are other crimes which would fail Lord Atkin's test, so, for example, if a person is wrongly accused of a parking violation this would hardly amount to defamation. How would you regard a person whom you believed had been convicted of failure to obtain a television license?

There are many examples of allegations of professional incompetence in the case law ranging from a doctor accused of "gross negligence" (*Simmers v Morton*) to a market gardener accused of letting weeds over-run his plots (*Cadzow v Edinburgh Distress Committee*). Allegations of professional misconduct differ slightly as they do not necessarily include any suggestion of incompetence. Such allegations are nonetheless damaging because of the pursuer's professional position. To accuse a person of being a racist might or might not be defamatory depending on the context. However, in *Fraser v Mirza* it was held defamatory to allege that a police officer was motivated by racism to arrest a person.

Allegations of financial unsoundness may offer no comment on the moral character of a person, but may nevertheless have negative consequences. The victim may no longer be able to obtain credit, credit already extended may be withdrawn. Allegations of this type are actionable as defamation, although there is some difficulty in reconciling this with the test which requires lowering in social esteem. It has been suggested that defamation operates to protect a person's commercial character as well as their private persona.

Politicians and persons in public office in general must bear a great deal of criticism and even abuse. Such elements are part and parcel of public life and the public has a legitimate interest in the criticism of public office bearers whom they either elect directly or who are appointed by elected persons or bodies. Depending on the circumstances there are a range of defences that may come into play. A distinction has to be drawn between attacks on public and private character. It may not be defamatory to criticise the way in which a council leader does their job, but it is defamatory to suggest that they are corrupt or enervated by base motives. In short the latitude given to criticism of the council leader *qua* public officer is not extended to criticism of the council leader *qua* individual.

It may be noted that s.106(1) of the Representation of the People Act 1983 makes it a criminal offence to make a false statement about the personal character or conduct of a candidate for parliament before or during an election. Any such charge may be defended if it can be shown that there were reasonable grounds for belief in the statement and that the accused did in fact believe it to be true. The offended politician must, however, reflect on whether either civil litigation or criminal proceedings are likely to turn out to their advantage.

DEFENCES TO DEFAMATION

Innocent defamation

Section 1(1) of the Defamation Act 1996 provides that a person has a defence if he shows that: a) he was not the author, editor or publisher of the statement b) he took reasonable care in relation to its publication and c) he did not know, and had no reason to know, that what he did caused or contributed to the publication of a defamatory statement. Section 1(2) and (3) provide interpretation on the meanings of author, editor or publisher, notably the originator of a statement is not the author if he or she did not intend it to be published. Those with no responsibility for publication such as persons involved in the production process or selling newspapers are protected by this defence. Those who do have responsibility for publication are only protected to the extent that they have taken reasonable care. Once informed that they are publishing defamatory material they will be liable if they fail to take action to remove it as occurred in *Godfrey v Demon Internet*.

Offer to make amends

The disseminator of a defamatory statement may make an offer of amends under s.2. This offer can be made whether the defamation has occurred innocently or not, but it does imply an admission of liability. An offer is made to correct the statement, publish an apology and pay compensation. Like any offer, it can be accepted or rejected. Acceptance ends proceedings, but s.3 makes provision for enforcement and for determination of terms not agreed upon. If the offer is rejected then the fact that one was made may be used as a defence under s.4. This defence precludes the use of other defences. This is a good defence provided the defender had no grounds for believing that the statement was defamatory of the pursuer. This, indeed, will be presumed to be the case, the onus falls on the pursuer to rebut the presumption by proving intent to injure, see s.4(3) and *Milne v Express Newspapers*.

Veritas

Since by definition a defamatory statement is untrue, *veritas* (truth) affords a complete defence. The onus is on the defender to prove the truth of the allegation. Under the Defamation Act 1952 s.5 the defender need only prove the truth of those facts which are defamatory, other facts, which do not materially affect the reputation of the pursuer need not be proved. When applied successfully this defence rebuts the presumption of falsity.

In rixa

Rixa means a quarrel or brawl. Words uttered in the heat of the moment may be defensible on grounds that they were not seriously intended. It follows that this defence is only available in respect of spoken and not written defamation. The classic example of this defence is *Christie v Robertson*. A misunderstanding arose at an auction when two men both thought they had bought the same horse. When one of them led it away a quarrel ensued in which one man said of the other that he "should have been in the hands of the police 20 times in the last five years". The defence succeeded. Similarly, in the colourful case of *Harper v Fernie* the female pursuer got no damages when called a "damned drunken old whore" during a heated altercation with a neighbour.

Vulgar abuse and sarcasm

Statements that are abusive or sarcastic are treated similarly to words uttered *in rixa*, they are not viewed as seriously intended. Thus great scope is allowed satirical television programmes, magazines and cartoons to lampoon public figures without fear of attracting litigation. Reasonable viewers or readers will not regard mockery or abuse as serious allegation. Similarly, football referees cannot seek damages in defamation in respect of statements questioning the marital status of their parents or suggesting severe visual impairment.

Fair retort

If an allegation is made against a person that person is entitled to reply. If the reply contains defamatory elements then it may found an action for defamation, but there is no presumption of malice because the motivation behind the statement is to protect the defender's own reputation. Therefore, where fair retort applies, the pursuer will have to prove intent to injure on the part of the defender. This may be seen, for example, in *Gray v SSPCA*, in which the defenders responded to an accusation of cruel injustice by repeating the substance of complaints they had brought against a farmer and in respect of which he had been prosecuted, but found not proven. The defenders also pointed out to the readership the difference between a not proven and guilty verdict. In order to count as a fair retort the reply must be kept within the bounds of relevance. In *Blair v Eastwood* the defender overstepped the boundaries of fair retort when he was accused by the pursuer of having fathered her child. He in turn accused the pursuer of having had sex with at least two other men. This was not a fair retort.

Fair comment

The defence of fair comment arises in the context of statements of opinion on matters in which the public has an interest. As a matter of policy the law allows considerable freedom of expression. The subject of the comment might be a government or party policy, it might be a statement by a minister or other politician, it might be a letter published in a newspaper, it might be in the form of a review of a book, a play, a painting, music or even a building. The defence is generally available in all circumstances where there is an element of public interest in informed criticism. The reading, listening or viewing public may make their own judgement on the validity of any comment when presented with the facts upon which the comment is made.

Reviews or comments may be scathing yet, provided certain criteria are met, they will not give rise to liability in defamation. As Lord McLaren stated in *Archer v Ritchie & Co*:

"The expression of an opinion as to a state of facts truly set forth is not actionable, even when that opinion is couched in vituperative or contumelious language."

In order for the defence to apply three criteria have to be met. First, the statement must be a comment on fact. Secondly, the facts must be truly stated. The Defamation Act 1952 s.6 provides that the defence will be good if the facts upon which the opinion is based are true even if there are other facts which are not true. Thirdly, the facts must concern some matter of public interest. The onus is on the defender to establish these three criteria. Once these criteria have been established the onus then passes to the pursuer to establish that the comment was made with the intent to injure.

Whether or not a comment is fair is determined by its relevance to the facts. Thus, for example, provided a book review does not misrepresent the content of the book, the reviewer is at liberty to state that the book is garbage. This is an opinion on a fact (the content of the book) and as such attracts the defence of fair comment. On the other hand, if the reviewer states that the author is illiterate and must have slept with the publisher in order to get into print, that goes beyond comment on the content of the book and will not be deemed fair.

Absolute privilege

Unlike fair comment the defence of privilege is not generally applicable. The defence of privilege is only available in certain circumstances where the public interest in freedom of speech over-rides any personal interest in reputation. Where statements are absolutely privileged they cannot found an action for defamation or verbal injury, irrespective of whether the communication is motivated by the intent to injure. Any action in defamation or verbal injury will be irrelevant. Absolute privilege applies to statements made in the Westminster Parliament, whether these are made by MPs or by others, such as witnesses before Select Committees. It also applies to reports and other papers issued under the authority of parliament including the reports of parliamentary proceedings in *Hansard*. Absolute privilege applies equally to proceedings before the Scottish Parliament and reports and papers authorised by it, by virtue of the Scotland Act 1998 s.41.

Judicial proceedings too attract absolute privilege, although here the protection afforded is less than in the case of parliamentary proceedings. Judges enjoy absolute privilege in the exercise of their judicial function. This privilege may be lost, however, in the event that a judge makes remarks that are not pertinent to the case before the court. This is in contrast to statements made in parliament, where a defamatory statement that has nothing whatsoever to do with the matter under consideration, is nonetheless absolutely privileged. It may be noted that parliament exercises its own discipline. The absolute privilege enjoyed by judges extends to inferior courts and tribunals as well as to supreme courts.

Similarly, advocates and solicitors are protected by absolute privilege, not only in respect of what is said in court, but also in respect of written pleadings. Like judges, this protection may be lost where a defamatory statement is made in circumstances that no reasonable person would view as connected with the matter in hand. Witnesses also enjoy absolute privilege in respect of statements made in evidence and also with regard to statements made to the police or in precognition. See, for example, *Bolam v Burns*. Again, privilege is lost where a witness makes statements that are not pertinent to the case. So long as witnesses confine themselves to answering questions put to them by the judge or by counsel, absolute privilege applies. In the event that some extraneous comment is made that has no bearing on the question posed, then privilege may be lost.

It should be noted that, in contrast to England, parties to civil litigation in Scotland enjoy only qualified privilege. The parties are present for their own benefit and not in the discharge of any public duty. The possibility of an action in defamation or verbal injury may serve to deter frivolous and vexatious litigation. Of course, if a party is called into the witness box by the opposition, the party is a witness and statements are absolutely privileged. The same does not apply in respect of evidence given by the party on their own behalf.

Members of juries enjoy absolute privilege. While in theory jurors also could lose absolute privilege by some irrelevant remark, there is little scope for such an occurrence and there is no case law on this point.

The protection afforded judicial proceedings extends also to quasi-judicial proceedings and tribunals, such as public enquiries, employment appeal tribunals and children's hearings.

It may be noted that absolute privilege has been granted by statute to reports and publications of parliamentary ombudsmen. Furthermore absolute privilege attaches to the Lord Advocate in connection with prosecutions on indictment and, in turn, to procurators fiscal and advocates depute acting in accordance with the Lord Advocate's instructions. Ministers of the Crown are afforded absolute privilege in the proper exercise of their functions.

The Defamation Act 1996 s.14 provides that fair and accurate reports of court proceedings published contemporaneously are absolutely privileged. A wide interpretation is given courts so that childrens' hearings, employment appeal tribunals and public enquiries are included along with all UK courts, the European Court of Justice, the European Court of Human Rights and International Criminal Tribunals.

Qualified privilege

Qualified privilege arises where a statement is made in response to a duty. The recipient of the communication must have an interest in hearing it. As Lord Atkinson stated in *Adam v Ward*:

> . "A privileged occasion is...an occasion where the person who makes a communication has an interest or a duty, legal, social or moral, to make it to the person to whom it is made, and the person to whom it is so made has a corresponding interest or duty to receive it. This reciprocity is essential"

Anything defamatory that is communicated may be presumed to be a genuine response to the duty rather than evidence of intent to injure. Where qualified privilege applies the pursuer must prove intent to injure.

Consider the following example. X makes an allegation to the police that Y is abusing his children. Y sues in defamation. X pleads qualified privilege. There is little doubt that X is under a social and moral duty to bring such a concern to the relevant authorities even though, strictly speaking X is under no legal obligation to report crime. The court agrees there is a duty, accordingly X's communication is privileged. If X's allegation is honestly made the defence succeeds, even though criminal investigation does not find evidence or sufficient evidence to conclude that the children have indeed been abused. If X's allegation is malicious then X will be liable in damages, but only if Y can prove intent to injure. One way Y could do this is to establish that his children live in South America, he has no contact with them and these facts are known to X. It follows that X could not have believed in the truth of her allegations and so intent to injure may be inferred. Had X made the allegation not to the police, but to other neighbours, qualified privilege would not apply. Unlike the police the neighbours have no legitimate interest in receiving the information.

The press and media in general have a duty to the public to inform. Certain types of reporting are accorded qualified privilege by the Defamation Act 1996 s.15 and Sch.1. The schedule contains a long list covering reports of the deliberations of various types of body including council committee meetings, associations for promoting sports, arts, sciences and so on.

The Reynolds defence of responsible journalism

Aside from circumstances in which privilege operates the media is given considerable protection by the defence of fair comment. Fair comment, however, depends on facts being accurately stated. *Veritas* depends on facts being true. The *Reynolds* defence operates, in the public interest in being informed, and in the interests of freedom of speech, to provide protection in circumstances where the publisher is uncertain of the facts. In *Reynolds v The Times Newspapers* certain defamatory allegations were published concerning the plaintiff who had just resigned as Taoiseach of the Republic of Ireland. The reasons for the resignation were clearly a matter of public interest and the defendants sought the extension of privilege to political information in general.

The House of Lords did not grant the defendants the defence asked for, but formulated something which was at first viewed as a development on privilege, but which has come to be seen as a new defence. The effect of the defence is that unproven allegations may be published where there is a duty to do so and a corresponding right on the part of the public to know. Where the defence applies it is not open to the pursuer to offer to prove intent to injure. This was established by the House of Lords in *Jameel v Wall Street Journal*. The conditions that have to be met for the defence to apply are such as to establish the propriety of the defender's behaviour and exclude malice.

A ten 10 point guide to the factors to be considered was set down by Lord Nicholls in *Reynolds*. Although there was an attempt, in *Loutchansky v Times Newspapers*, to have these factors treated as strict tests, the Court of Appeal in that case made it clear that they were not to be applied in that way, but were factors indicating the ingredients of "responsible journalism" Lord Nicholls' guide follows:

"Depending on the circumstances, the matters to be taken into account include the following. The comments are illustrative only. 1. The seriousness of the allegation. The more serious the charge, the more the public is misinformed and the individual harmed, if the allegation is not true. 2. The nature of the information, and the extent to which the subject matter is a matter of public concern. 3. The source of the information. Some informants have no direct knowledge of the events. Some have their own axes to grind, or are being paid for their stories. 4. The steps taken to verify the information. 5. The status of the information. The allegation may have already been the subject of an investigation which commands respect. 6. The urgency of the matter. News is often a perishable commodity. 7. Whether comment was sought from the plaintiff. He may have information others do not possess or have not disclosed. An approach to the plaintiff will not always be necessary. 8. Whether the article contained the gist of the plaintiff's side of the story. 9. The tone of the article. A newspaper can raise queries or call for an investigation. It need not adopt allegations as statements of fact. The circumstances of the publication, including the timing."

The *Reynolds* defence is proving a fertile ground of legal development. It has been applied in Scotland in *Adams v Guardian Newspapers Ltd*. The defence is not restricted to the media. In the Privy Council case *Seaga v Harper* it was held it might apply to any person publishing in a medium, but of course, its applicability is subject to the extent to which the conditions set out by Lord Nicholls are met.

VERBAL INJURY

The critical differences between defamation and verbal injury may be simply stated. Verbal injury is the appropriate form of action where a reputation has been harmed by words, spoken or written, that are not defamatory. The form of *culpa* that is relevant for liability is malice, but, unlike defamation, malice is not presumed. As the statement is not defamatory there is no basis for any such presumption. Therefore malice must be averred and proved. Furthermore, a verbal injury is not actionable unless the statement complained of is false. Again, because the statement is not defamatory there is no basis for a presumption of falsity. Accordingly the onus lies on the pursuer to prove that the statement complained of is false.

Verbal injury as distinct from defamation developed out of cases brought by public figures (at least in the local context) such as teachers, ministers and politicians. The basis for complaint was that statements had held them up to public odium, or hatred, contempt and ridicule. The requirements for actionability as outlined in the preceding paragraph were established in 1893 in *Paterson v Welch* and confirmed more recently in *Steele v Scottish Daily Record and Sunday Mail Ltd*. Where it can be shown that a false statement was intended to hold the subject up to hatred, contempt and ridicule, damages in the form of solatium are available. Likewise any patrimonial loss is recoverable in damages.

Other forms of verbal injury include slander of title, slander of property and slander of business. Slander of title is a false imputation that a person does not own property that is being sold. An example of slander of property is a statement that a building is in danger of collapsing as in *Bruce v JM Smith*. Such a statement would have the effect of reducing the value or selling price of the property or limiting the market to those interested in the purchase of insecure buildings. Slander of business might be constituted by a statement that a business is incompetently run or is not in a position to meet its liabilities. It can be seen that in none of these situations is the allegation prima facie defamatory in the sense of lowering the esteem of the victim in the views of right thinking people, nevertheless considerable harm may be done. The nature of the harm done is most likely to be economic and so, provided it can be shown that the statement is false and that the words were calculated to cause pecuniary loss, damages for patrimonial loss will be available. It will not be necessary to prove actual pecuniary loss by virtue of s.3 of the Defamation Act 1952. Since the loss is economic rather than affront, communication of the statement to a third party will be required.

---

7. STATUTORY LIABILITY

INTRODUCTION

The other chapters in this book have been concerned primarily with the common law. In this chapter delictual liability arising from statute is briefly considered.

First, requirements relating to statutory negligence in general are outlined. Two sections follow in which particular forms of statutory liability are considered. These are occupiers' liability and liability for animals.

STATUTORY NEGLIGENCE

A claim in negligence may arise in respect of a duty imposed upon the defender by an Act of Parliament. While in such cases it is clearly not necessary to establish the existence of a duty by reference to the neighbourhood principle, proceeding on the basis of statutory duty casts up its own complications.

Where a statute imposes a duty on a party this does not automatically give the pursuer a right to litigate on the basis of the provision. It must be established that the Act contemplates civil liability in the event of breach. In some Acts it is expressly stated that breach gives rise to civil liability. Section 1 of the Occupiers' Liability (Scotland) Act 1960 is an example. In other Acts civil liability is specifically excluded, for example, by the Health and Safety at Work Act 1974 s.47.

Where the Act is silent on whether civil litigation is to be competent the need for construction arises. Taking into account the whole statute, the pre-existing law, the scope and purpose of the statute and for whose benefit the duty was intended, courts seek to determine the intention of Parliament. This process of construction can be seen in the case of *Cutler v Wandsworth Stadium Ltd (in liquidation)*. A bookmaker raised an action for damages against a licensed dog track in respect of their refusal to allow him space on their premises to carry on his trade. He founded on the Betting and Lotteries Act 1934 s.11(2), which imposed on dog track operators a duty to make space available for bookmakers on the track. It was determined in the House of Lords, upholding the decision in the Court of Appeal, that this provision concerned the regulation of the way in which places of amusement were to be managed. Accordingly, the provision was intended to benefit the public at large and not bookmakers in particular. While the duty had been breached, this did not entitle the plaintiff to found on s.11 in a civil action. Where there is doubt regarding whether recourse to civil action is permissible, courts will not allow such action in circumstances where the provision was not clearly intended to benefit the pursuer. A further example may be found in *Pullar v Window Clean Ltd*. Following the decision of the House of Lords in *Gorringe v Calderdale MBC*, a party who has failed to establish a case based on breach of statutory duty cannot then seek to improve their chances of success by falling back on the common law.

Where civil action is competent, recovery in damages will only be possible where the loss incurred reflects the harm against which parliament sought to legislate. A very clear example is provided by the case of *Gorris v Scott*, in which a statutory duty requiring the shippers of livestock to keep the animals penned in transit was breached. The plaintiff's sheep were swept overboard on voyage. The plaintiff was unable to recover damages since the purpose of the duty was to prevent contagion of disease.

Just as in common law cases, it must be shown that the duty was breached and that the loss was caused by the breach. Unlike the common law in which the standard of care is always the standard of the reasonable man, statute commonly imposes higher standards. Liability may be absolute in the sense that there is no scope for defending a breach and it may be strict in the sense that pursuers are not required to prove fault on the part of defenders. Equally the standard of care may be set at a similar level to the common law. Such is the case in the Occupiers' Liability (Scotland) Act 1960 s.2(1). The standard of care applicable depends on the wording of the statute.

Where a statute imposes absolute liability, evidence of the degree of care taken to avoid the breach will not be relevant in defence. For example, s.22(1) of the Factories Act 1937 provides, "[e]very hoist or lift shall be of good mechanical construction, sound material and adequate strength, and be properly maintained". In *Millar v Galashiels Gas Co Ltd* a workman was killed through the failure of the brake mechanism on a hoist and an action for damages was brought, founding on s.22(1). Every possible step had been taken to ensure the proper working and safety of the mechanism. The failure was unexplained and could not have been anticipated. Nevertheless, the House of Lords found the defenders in breach of a duty and therefore liable in damages.

Part 1 of the Consumer Protection Act 1987 imposes strict liability on producers for property damage or personal injury arising from defective products. Consumers may recover compensation without any need to prove negligence or fault on the part of defenders.

Where claims are pursued on the basis of breach of statutory duty, the defence *volenti non fit injuria* is in general inapplicable. Of course, where this defence is expressly provided for in the statute it applies. For example, s.2(3) of the Occupiers' Liability (Scotland) Act 1960 provides for the application of *volenti*. The defence of contributory negligence is generally available.

EXERCISE OF DISCRETION BY PUBLIC BODIES

Ministers of the Crown, local authorities and other government agencies exercise powers under statute. The statutory powers such bodies are given commonly involve the exercise of discretion. Where discretion is exercised carelessly to the detriment of an individual, that person can, in principle, seek reparation under the common law. In such a case it is necessary to establish that a duty of care was owed to the pursuer in accordance with the normal common law rules of negligence. There has to be foreseeability of harm, proximity must be established and it has to be fair, just and reasonable before courts will hold that a duty was owed. However, courts have demonstrated reluctance to recognise duties in such circumstances. So, for example, in *Harris v Evans* a local authority acted on the advice of a health and safety inspector exercising statutory powers regarding a mobile crane used for bungee jumping. The business was closed down for some time. The pursuers, who had lost profits during this period, were unable to establish that a duty of care was owed them by the inspector. Duties of care were, however, recognised in *Gibson v Chief Constable of Strathclyde* and *Burnett v Grampian Fire Services* as discussed in Chapter 2.

Two types of situation may be identified. First, where a body has discretion on broad policy issues no duty will arise from the way in which that discretion is exercised unless, following *Hallett v Nicholson* and *Bonthrone v Secretary of State for Scotland*, it can be shown that the authority acted in bad faith. So, for example, if X suffers food poisoning in a local hotel and attribute this to the fact that the local authority no longer spends sufficient amounts on environmental health, having exercised its discretion to spend more on recreation and amenities instead, this will not be a competent basis for civil action. Even though the hotel has not been subjected to an environmental health inspection, broad policy decisions exercised in good faith are not justiciable.

The second type of situation arises where discretion is exercised at an operational level. Principles of administrative law come into play so no liability will arise from the exercise of that discretion, unless it is exercised in such an unreasonable fashion that no authority acting reasonably could have exercised discretion in that way. For example, NHS 24 prioritises ambulance calls. If X calls for an ambulance for a relative who is suffering chest pain and the available ambulance is directed first to attend a road traffic accident, no liability will arise even though the relative dies from a heart attack and the victims of the road accident turn out to have no more than superficial wounds. In *Kent v Griffiths* on the other hand it was held an ambulance crew owed a duty to arrive on the scene of an accident within a reasonable time. Having accepted the call they had assumed responsibility and were liable in damages when the plaintiff suffered brain damage as a result of their delay. In this case no alternative demands were being made on the crew at the time.

In *Stovin v Wise* the local authority had statutory powers to remove dangers from roads though they were not under any statutory duty to do so. The House of Lords held by a majority that no common law duty was owed when a motorcyclist suffered serious injury when a car pulled across his path. The driver's view had been obscured by a bank which was known to the authority to make the junction dangerous. Similarly in *Gorringe v Calderdale* there was no common law duty to paint warning signs on a road although the local authority had the power to do so.

HUMAN RIGHTS

Public bodies are obliged by the Human Rights Act 1998 to give effect to those rights specified by the European Convention. Litigation brought in respect of human rights is giving rise to an increasing body of case law. Even before the enactment of the Human Rights Act the UK was taken to the European Court of Human Rights by a mother and son called Osman, alleging breach of Art.6, the right to a fair trial. In *Osman v Ferguson* the plaintiff's claim against the police had been struck out on policy grounds. The parties sued in respect of negligent failure to apprehend a schoolteacher who had become obsessed with the boy, lost his job and who conducted a campaign of harassment before eventually wounding the boy and shooting his father dead. Clearly the proximity element that had denied liability in

Hill v Constable of West Yorkshire could be satisfied here, but the claim was struck out on the same policy ground as applied in *Hill*. The judgment of the Court of Appeal did, however, make it look as if a blanket immunity was being granted the police and damages were awarded in *Osman v UK*. In the subsequent case of *Z v UK* the European Court of Human Rights accepted that they had been mistaken in *Osman*. Though *Osman* is discredited it has had the effect that courts have to be very clear that policy is an integral part of the *Caparo* test and to avoid any suspicion of the application of blanket immunities. *Z v UK* establishes that Art.6 is not breached simply because a duty of care was denied provided that the litigant had the opportunity to argue that in the circumstances it was fair, just and reasonable to recognise a duty.

Article 6 secures the right to have a claim relating to a party's civil rights brought before a civil court, but *Roche v UK* affirms that the content of such rights must be determined according to the laws of the domestic jurisdiction.

Z v UK was the appeal from *X (Minors) v Bedfordshire County Council*. In this case the House of Lords heard five separate appeals. The first two were claims that the local authority had failed to take children into care despite evidence of abuse and that one child had been wrongfully taken into care, the remaining three concerned failure on the part of the local authorities to identify learning difficulties or had failed to make adequate provision for schooling. The abuse cases were struck out on *Caparo* rules, that it would not be fair, just and reasonable to impose a duty of care on the social workers and psychologists making decisions on children's welfare. The education cases were allowed to go to trial. *Z v UK* was brought in respect of the children who had not been taken into care. The European Court of Human Rights found that Art.3, prohibition of torture or inhuman and degrading treatment and Art.13, right to compensation in the event of a violation of one of the substantive rights, were breached. Subsequently, in *Barrett v Enfield LBC* the House of Lords distinguished *X v Bedfordshire* and found a common law duty of care owed to a child taken into care to guard against personal injuries. In *D v East Berkshire Community Health NHS Trust* claims were brought by parents and in one case a child in respect of psychiatric harm caused by wrongful allegations of child abuse. The claims brought by parents were dismissed in the Court of Appeal but, in a departure from *X v Bedfordshire*, the claim brought by the child was allowed to proceed. The policy reason for denying the parents' claim was given by Lord Phillips MR: "where child care decisions are being taken, no common law duty of care should be owed to the parents." This identifies the potential conflict of interest that would be caused by having to consider parents in circumstances where the welfare of the child is paramount. The decision of the Court of Appeal was upheld by a majority in the House of Lords and an attempt to revisit the same issue in a subsequent case, *Lawrence v Pembrokeshire County Council*, merely resulted in affirmation of the policy stance taken in *D v East Berkshire*.

Similar reasoning was employed in *Jain v Trent Strategic Health Authority* in which the claimants were denied a duty of care on the basis that this would create a conflict of interest when the authority exercised statutory powers to act in protection of elderly persons resident in the claimant's nursing home. The authority had cancelled the claimant's registration believing the home to be in an unacceptable condition due to building works, though this turned out not to be the case and the claimants suffered substantial economic loss.

OCCUPIERS' LIABILITY

Liability for negligence arising from defective premises or dangers on land is governed by the Occupiers' Liability (Scotland) Act 1960. In fact liability under this statute is not restricted to heritable property, but is extended by s.1(3)(a) to include "any fixed or moveable structure, including any vessel, vehicle or aircraft, and to persons entering thereon". For example, if a passenger in your car dies from carbon monoxide poisoning because the seal on the exhaust manifold leaks and exhaust gasses enter the passenger compartment, the case against you would proceed on the basis of the Act.

The Act imposes a duty on occupiers or those having control. This may be the owner, equally the property may be let and the tenant will be the person in occupation. The landlord will not be the person upon whom the duty is imposed unless they are responsible under the terms of the lease for maintenance or care of the premises (s.3(1)). If the premises are unoccupied then generally the owner will be subject to the duty since the owner has control. Broadly, the duty lies on the party with effective control. Identification of this party is governed by the common law by virtue of s.1(2).

The duty imposed by the Act is set out in s.2(1):

> "The care which an occupier of premises is required, by reason of his occupation or control of the premises, to show towards a person entering thereon in respect of dangers which are due to the state of the premises or to anything done or omitted to be done on them and for which the occupier is in law responsible shall, except in so far as he is entitled to and does restrict, modify or exclude by agreement his obligations towards that person, be such care as in all the circumstances of the case is reasonable to see that that person will not suffer injury or damage by reason of any such danger."

It must be noted that liability is not strict, the onus is on the pursuer to establish that the defender was at fault. A recent attempt to argue that a bouncer at a nightclub was a danger within the meaning of the Act failed in *Honeybourne v Burgess*.

The next point to note is that the standard of care imposed is that which is reasonable in the circumstances. The standard depends on the circumstances so the occupier is obliged to go to greater lengths to guard against hidden dangers than against obvious ones since the nature of the danger may be taken into account in determining the standard of care applicable. So far as injury caused by obvious dangers is concerned a pursuer may be deemed to have assented to the risk (s.2(3)). So, for example, there is no duty on a landowner to fence a fast flowing burn. A visitor to the land may be deemed to have assented to the risk if she attempts to cross and is drowned. However, this point depends on the type of person who may foreseeably enter the land. If it is foreseeable that very young children will enter the land unaccompanied then this alters the circumstances and the standard of care owed them is greater than it would be in respect of adults. In *Tomlinson v Congleton BC* the view that there is no duty to guard against natural hazards was recently reaffirmed.

A duty is owed persons who enter the land or premises and it does not matter whether such persons are entitled to be there or not. Accordingly a duty of care is owed to trespassers. However, the duty may be considered discharged if trespassers have to overcome an obvious hurdle to gain access such as a locked door or high fence. A trespasser cannot break into a lockfast building and then sue under the Act if he is then injured when a rotten floor gives way beneath his feet. On the other hand a trespasser who falls into a bear pit, is caught in a gin trap or mutilated by a landmine will have recourse to the law. For examples of cases involving trespassers and discussion on the way in which the standard of care owed is affected by the age of the pursuer see: *McGlone v British Railways Board*; *Titchener v British Railways Board*; and *Devlin v Strathclyde Regional Council*. In none of these cases was there held to be liability because the injured parties were old enough to appreciate the dangers to which they exposed themselves and they were, accordingly, *volens* of the risk. For example, the 14-year-old victim in *Devlin* was playing tig on a school roof when he decided to bounce off a skylight window from a height of some five feet. More recently in *McLeod v British Railways Board* a slightly different approach can be seen. In that case a 12-year-old boy fell on power cables carrying 25,000 volts. He spent nine months in hospital undergoing 10 skin graft operations. The defender was found liable with a 20 per cent reduction in damages for contributory negligence.

A further point to note is that the duty imposed by the Act may be modified or excluded by agreement. Where the premises in question are "business premises" any such modification is subject to the Unfair Contract Terms Act 1977 s.16, which renders any attempt to exclude or limit liability in respect of personal injury or death void. Other terms are subject to a test of reasonableness. Business (and therefore business premises) is widely defined in s.25(1) and covers government bodies, public authorities and professions, as well as manufacturers, retailers and service providers. Contracts allowing persons to enter onto land are expressly covered by the Act (s.15(2)(d) and (e)). In order to be effective to exclude or limit occupiers' liability, terms have to be very carefully drafted in accordance with common law rules on the construction of exemption clauses.

Finally, the standard of care imposed by the Occupiers' Liability (Scotland) Act does not detract from or relieve the occupier of liability in respect of any other duty imposed on particular premises or types of premises by any other statute or rule of law (s.2(2)).

LIABILITY FOR ANIMALS

The Animals (Scotland) Act 1987 imposes strict liability; that is liability without any requirement on the pursuer to prove *culpa*, on the keepers of certain animals in certain circumstances. Under the pre-existing common law, the keepers of animals *ferae naturae* (of a wild disposition) were presumed to know of the animal's dangerous propensities and were strictly liable for harm resulting from a failure to confine or control the animal. The keepers of animals *mansuetae naturae* (of a gentle disposition) were liable only if it could be proved either that they were aware of the particular animal's dangerous propensities or if they were negligent. The Act supersedes the common law strict liability regime. The old distinction between animals *ferae naturae* and *mansuetae naturae* has become redundant. However, common law actions may still be raised in negligence where harm is caused by animals. The normal rules of negligence apply and the fact that the agent of harm is an animal is largely irrelevant.

Under the Act strict liability attaches to the keeper of the animal, as defined in s.5. The keeper is the person who owns the animal or is in possession of it or, where the animal is owned by a child below the age of 16, the keeper is the person with actual care and control of the child. The owner remains the keeper of an abandoned animal. Section 3 allows the occupier of land onto which the animal has strayed to detain it. Where this right is exercised the person detaining the animal does not become the keeper.

Strict liability is imposed on the keeper in the event that the animal causes injury or damage (s.1(1)). However, not all animals are covered by the Act and not all types of harm or injury caused by those animals give rise to liability under the Act.

Section 1(1)(b) provides that keepers shall be liable if:

"[T]he animal belongs to a species whose members generally are by virtue of their physical attributes or habits likely (unless controlled or restrained) to injure severely or kill persons or animals, or damage property to a material extent and (c) the injury or damage complained of is directly referable to such physical attributes or habits."

Stated broadly, strict liability then follows only when either a fierce animal kills or causes injury by an attack or a foraging animal causes property harm through foraging. It will not arise where a fierce animal causes property harm or where a foraging animal causes personal injury. Thus, there is no liability under the Act if a wolf digs up a potato bed or if a person is ravaged by a sheep. In *Fairlie v Curruthers* the pursuer alleged she had been knocked down by a frisky dog. Since the dog had brushed against her and had not attacked or harried her there was no liability under the Act.

Section 1(1) operates subject to s.1(4) and (5), so liability under the Act does not arise where either the injury "consists of disease transmitted by means which are unlikely to cause severe injury other than disease" or where injury or damage is caused by "the mere fact that an animal is present on a road or other place".

This means that a farmer will not be strictly liable if foot and mouth disease spreads from his herd to other animals. Liability will arise where rabies is transmitted through a dog bite since a bite may cause severe injury. Where, as sometimes happens, a cow escapes from a field and causes a road accident there will be no liability under the Act. This is demonstrated in *Bennett v Lamont & Sons*. In situations where liability does not arise under the Act there may be liability at common law, but the pursuer will have to prove negligence or some other form of *culpa*.

Some of the animals covered by the Act are specified. Thus under s.1(3) dogs and all animals within the meaning of s.7(4) of the Dangerous Wild Animals Act 1976 are included on the basis that they are deemed likely, in the absence of control or restraint, to "injure severely or kill persons or animals by biting or otherwise savaging, attacking or harrying". The Schedule of the 1976 Act provides a long list of such animals that includes crocodiles, coral snakes, tigers and wolves. Other animals are listed in the 1987 Act s.1(3)(b), on the basis that they are likely to cause property damage, particularly to crops, when foraging. The animals thus specified are "cattle, horses, asses, mules, hinnies, sheep, pigs, goats and deer". It must be noted that the absence of a particular animal from any of these statutory lists does not exclude that animal from coverage by the Act. Any animal could be included provided it fits within the definition in s.1(1)(b).In *Foskett v McClymont* the question whether a bull is a species liable to injure was allowed to go to proof. This was a question of fact to be demonstrated by appropriate evidence. Viruses, bacteria, algae, fungi and protozoa are specifically excluded by virtue of s.7. According to accepted biological taxonomy none of these are, in any sense, animals.

Liability imposed by the Act is strict, it is not absolute so there are a number of defences provided for by s.2. No liability arises under the Act if the harm sustained was wholly due to the fault of the victim or the keeper of another animal where that animal is the victim. Furthermore, the defence of *volenti non fit injuria* is available in both these circumstances.

As noted under occupiers' liability a duty of care is owed to trespassers. Section 2(1)(c) of the 1987 Act provides a defence where a person or animal is injured when trespassing on the keeper's land. In such circumstances, while there may be liability based on fault under the Occupiers' Liability (Scotland) Act, the keeper is relieved of strict liability under the Animals (Scotland) Act. However, where the animal causing the injury is on the land "wholly or partly for the purposes of protecting persons or property" then the s.2(1)(c) defence is disapplied by s.2(2). Liability will be strict unless the use made of the guard animal was reasonable and if the animal is a guard dog, the use made of the dog must comply with s.1 of the Guard Dogs Act 1975. Compliance with this provision requires guard dogs to be under the control of their handlers or secured so that they cannot roam freely about the premises. Moreover, warning notices must be exhibited at every entrance to the premises.

Thus, if I trespass through a field and am gored by a bull, liability will not be strict assuming that the bull has not been placed in the field to act as a guard. I will have to prove negligence or some other form of *culpa* on the part of the defender. If I climb over a garden wall and I'm mauled by a jaguar let loose in the garden to act as a guard, then liability will be strict since the use of a jaguar as a guard animal is not reasonable. If I enter a scrapyard and am bitten by a guard dog roaming the premises outwith the control of a handler then liability will be strict. On the other hand, if the dog is chained up and there are warning notices at all entrances then I will not recover damages unless I can establish *culpa*.

A complication arises from the case of *Welsh v Brady*. The facts were very similar to *Fairlie v Carruthers*. A woman was knocked down and injured by a black labrador. This was not an attack, savaging or harrying. The pursuer argued that there could be strict liability under s.1(1)(b) if it could be shown that black labradors are, by virtue of their physical attributes or habits, likely to injure severely or kill persons or animals unless controlled or restrained. The pursuer was allowed to lead evidence, but it was not sufficient to support the contention and so the case was dismissed. This decision was later affirmed in the Inner House. The argument pursued here seems based on reading s.1(1) and (3) separately rather than together. While s.1(3)(a) refers to severe injury killing by biting, savaging, attacking or harrying, s.1(1)(b) refers to severe injury or killing without further specification. Rather than viewing s.1(3) as explanatory of s.1(1) the pursuers argument suggests these provisions provide separate bases for liability. Whether this reflects the intention of Parliament must be doubtful.

---

8. NUISANCE

INTRODUCTION

Nuisance emerged as a doctrine of Scots common law during the mid-eighteenth century. Prior to this the term "annoyance" was used to refer to such things as blocked drains, overflowing middens, foul effluent and so on, and such complaints were dealt with by inferior local courts such as the Dean of Guild court, burgh magistrates or barony courts. Nuisance in the common law of England law has a longer and better documented history, dating back to the twelfth century. There are important differences between the jurisdictions. In Scots law no distinction is drawn between public and private nuisance. Nuisance in Scots law is and always has been relatively narrow in scope—the term has never been applied to the broad range of circumstances described in England as "nuisances". The *plus quam tolerabile* test, which is determinant of nuisance in Scots law, is unique to this jurisdiction. In Scotland nuisance is always determined on a balance of interests between the parties. This is not the case in England where nuisance may be sub-divided into different forms, in some of which balancing interests is not a relevant means of proceeding (*Hunter v Canary Wharf*).

Finally, Scots law takes a distinctive approach to determining the basis for liability in reparation. Following the House of Lords case of *Strathclyde Regional Council v RHM Bakeries (Scotland) Ltd*, liability in reparation in respect of nuisance proceeds on the basis of *culpa*. Prior to *RHM* there had been a lengthy period in which liability was argued to be strict. While this issue was resolved in *RHM*, the case did not serve to differentiate nuisance from negligence. As Lord President Hope stated in the First Division in *Kennedy v Glenbelle*:

> "But the analysis of the authorities in that case did not go into the difficult question as to what types of delictual conduct on the part of the defender, amounting to *culpa* or fault on his part, are actionable on the ground of nuisance and what types are actionable by reference to the ordinary principles of negligence."

Such an analysis was conducted in *Kennedy*. Lord Hope reviewed the concept of *culpa* in the context of liability in reparation generally. It is clear from this analysis that where harm is caused unintentionally, "the ordinary principles of negligence will provide an equivalent remedy". In short, if the form taken by *culpa* is negligence then an action to recover damages should be grounded on negligence. The relevant form of *culpa* in an action for damages grounded on nuisance is intention or recklessness. In *Kennedy* an averment of "a deliberate act done in the knowledge that harm would be the likely result" was held to be a relevant averment of *culpa* in an action for damages grounded on nuisance.

This means that nuisance can be seen as a delict of intention. *Culpa* is inferred from a deliberate act done in the knowledge that harm will almost certainly follow. Knowledge of the harm that will follow is viewed constructively. This is affirmed in the later case of *Anderson v White*. The issue is not what the defender actually knew, but what ought to have been apparent to a reasonable person in the position of the defender. Doing something, while knowing that it is going to cause harm, is not negligent, but intentional. Harm need not be a desired consequence, it is sufficient for intentional liability if harm is a more or less inevitable consequence.

If nuisance is seen as a delict of intention then this has great advantages for the general coherence of the doctrine. On coherence, one critical point is that nuisance is established on the *plus quam tolerabile* test. This test measures the gravity of the harm. The test is a mechanism whereby the court considers whether the invasion of the pursuer's right to comfortable enjoyment of their property is sufficiently serious to amount in law to nuisance. If the harm is greater than a reasonable proprietor could be expected to tolerate then nuisance is established. If, in addition, *culpa* is established then there is liability in reparation for nuisance.

It has been argued strongly by Professor Whitty in the *Stair Memorial Encyclopaedia* (see "Nuisance", paras 17, 77, 89, 104–106) that the *plus quam tolerabile* test is inapplicable in cases of unintentional harm. This is because in unintentional harm cases potential gravity of harm is taken into account at a different stage in determining whether or not a duty of care arises. If liability for negligent acts were to be determined on the *plus quam tolerabile* test then, in cases where the harm was material, the test would always be positive and there would always be liability, even in circumstances where the risk of material harm was so slight that the defender was entitled to ignore it. This would impose strict liability contrary to the rule in *RHM*. By regarding nuisance as a delict of intention this problem is averted and it is clear that the *plus quam tolerabile* requirement is applicable in every case of nuisance as it was originally intended to be.

Nonetheless, while there are nuisance cases subsequent to *Kennedy*, such as *Anderson v White* and *Powrie Castle Properties v Dundee City Council*, in which *culpa* is averred in terms of "a deliberate act done in the knowledge that harm would be the likely result", there is one case, the *Globe (Aberdeen) Ltd v North of Scotland Water Authority*, in which *culpa* was averred in terms that appear much more like negligence, and in one further case, *British Waterways Board v Moore & Mulheron Contracts Ltd*, the sheriff clearly viewed negligence as a relevant form of *culpa* in an action grounded on nuisance. Most recently, in *Viewpoint Housing Association Ltd v The City of Edinburgh* the pursuers founded alternative claims of nuisance and negligence on the same pleadings of *culpa*. We can conclude that, while there is clear authority to support the view that intention and recklessness are relevant forms of *culpa* in a nuisance action and negligence is not, this point is perhaps not yet fully accepted. The issue turns on the proper interpretation to be given the opinion of Lord Hope in *Kennedy v Glenbelle*. Since Lord Hope explicitly set out to differentiate between the forms of *culpa* actionable on grounds of nuisance and those in negligence, it is hard to believe that he could have intended to leave the incoherent notion of the negligent nuisance intact.

From *RHM* a possible exception arises to the general rule that liability depends on *culpa* where property harm has followed alterations on the course of a natural stream. The relevant authority is the House of Lords case of *Caledonian Railway Co v Greenock Corporation*. This case was long understood to be an authority that supported strict liability for property harm. *Caledonian* was distinguished and not over-ruled in *RHM*. The case may best be regarded as misunderstood, because it is badly reported. The unreported parts of the case, particularly the opinion of Lord Dewar in the Outer House, show that the pursuers succeeded in establishing the fault of the defenders at first instance. The view that *Caledonian* supports a doctrine of strict liability must therefore be highly doubtful. Nevertheless, this issue was also raised in *Viewpoint* with both parties appearing to accept that alterations on the course of a natural stream could give rise to strict liability. Since the issue was not raised properly in pleadings no ruling was made on the point. Subsequently, in *Bloom v Russell* the pursuer withdrew pleadings on strict liability in response to a preliminary plea tabled by the defenders in which Lord Dewar's opinion in *Caledonian* was cited as authority.

THE NATURE OF NUISANCE

Nuisance by its nature normally arises between neighbours, although it is not the case that properties must be adjoining even though nuisance has at times been described as operating between adjoining proprietors. The essence of nuisance is that the defender is carrying out some activity on their land that interferes with the comfortable enjoyment of the pursuer's property, because the activity causes discomfort or inconvenience. However, it is not a legal requirement that the source of harm is on land owned or occupied by the defender. In *Allison v Stevenson* a lady was interdicted from feeding pigeons in the street. The droppings blocked the pursuers' roans and drainpipes.

Up until the end of the nineteenth century, nuisance in Scotland was concerned almost exclusively with what may broadly be termed as pollution. Thus actions were brought in respect of pollution of water and air, in respect of unusual noise, unnatural heat and vibration. Examples include *Dowie v Oliphant*, in which the boiling of whale blubber was interdicted because of the unwholesome smell, and *Johnston v Constable*, in which the alleged nuisance was a steam engine operating in a tenement causing heat and vibration.

Dangers, when they materialised and harm resulted, tended to give rise to reparation actions grounded on negligence rather than nuisance. Prospective and present dangers, such as fire hazards, on the other hand, could be interdicted in nuisance as occurred in *Vary v Thomson*. Interdict was granted against a blacksmith's operation in the vicinity of thatched houses. It remains the case that a dangerous state of affairs may be the subject of a court order. In *Canmore Housing Association v Bairnsfather* the petitioner was unable to obtain an interim remedy under s.47(2) of the Court of Session Act 1988. The petitioner sought to have the respondent ordered to remove derelict cars parked against its property, but failed because materiality of risk was not established. Where a material risk of material harm is established then a remedy ought to be available.

Almost all eighteenth and nineteenth century nuisance cases were actions for interdict. People found life in their homes intolerable because of, for instance, smoke or noise. Reparation was sought in nuisance in only a handful of cases in which physical harm to property was consequent upon either air or water pollution. In more recent times the relative proportions of interdict to reparation cases has changed. Between 1976 and 2000 there were twice as many actions for reparation reported as those for interdict. Traditional nuisance actions to interdict polluting activities declined as a consequence of Municipal Improvement and Public Health legislation and planning regimes so that during the twentieth century such cases became infrequent. Planning meant that polluting processes were less likely to occur in residential areas, and new regulatory regimes and public health legislation meant that where nuisance did arise it could be dealt with by means other than the common law. Moreover, during the early twentieth century nuisance came to be understood as an infringement of a property right rather than as a state of affairs itself. This allowed for expansion of the scope of nuisance so that material harm to property has come to be understood as nuisance, whether or not it is consequent upon pollution. In practise this expansion in scope has been limited to property harm caused through flooding and deprivation of support for buildings. Nuisance, however, need no longer be limited in scope by the way in which the harm is caused. It is thought, following *Kennedy v Glenbelle*, that nuisance is the appropriate ground of action wherever material property harm amounting to nuisance is caused intentionally.

It is important to note that while *culpa* must be shown in cases where damages are sought this is not the case in actions for interdict. To obtain an interdict it is necessary to establish nuisance, it is not necessary to prove *culpa*.

Nuisance has sometimes been described as a continuing state of affairs rather than an isolated event. In the normal case this is a fair description, indeed interdict will only be awarded in respect of a source of disturbance or harm that is anticipated to either continue or take place in the future. However, it is perfectly clear that damages may be sought in respect of a one off event, such as flooding from a burst sewer, so while a continuing state of affairs is the normal case in nuisance, it is not a requirement for an award of damages.

ESTABLISHING NUISANCE

The right protected by the doctrine of nuisance is the right to comfortable enjoyment of property, free from serious disturbance, substantial inconvenience or material harm. The modern authority on the constitution of nuisance in Scots law is *Watt v Jamieson*.

In order to obtain a remedy against an interference with the right to comfortable enjoyment it is necessary to establish that the invasion amounts to nuisance. This is achieved by application of the *plus quam tolerabile* test. Nuisance is considered from the standpoint of the victim. Taking relevant circumstances into consideration the court must consider whether the interference to which the victim is exposed is *plus quam tolerabile*, that is more than reasonably tolerable. An action cannot be defended solely on the ground that the defender's activities are reasonable, although this is a factor that may be taken into account in balancing the interests of the parties. As Lord President Cooper stated in *Watt*:

> "[I]f any person so uses his property as to occasion serious disturbance or substantial inconvenience to his neighbour or material damage to his neighbour's property, it is in the general case irrelevant to plead merely that he was making a normal and familiar use of his own property. The balance in all such cases has to be held between the freedom of a proprietor to use his property as he pleases and the duty on a proprietor not to inflict material loss or inconvenience on adjoining proprietors and adjoining property; and in every case the answer depends on considerations of fact and degree... The critical question is whether what he was exposed to

was *plus quam tolerabile* when due weight has been given to all the surrounding circumstances of the offensive conduct and its effects."

The relevant circumstances that may be taken into consideration in the process of balancing the parties' interests may be summarised as follows. On the pursuer's side it is relevant to consider: the type of harm; the extent of the harm; the social value of the use or enjoyment invaded; the suitability of that use to the locality; the sensitivity to harm of the pursuer or property affected; and the burden on the pursuer of implementing protective measures. On the defender's side it is relevant to consider: the primary purpose of the conduct or operation; the suitability of the operation to the locality; and the practicability of remedial measures.

RELEVANT FACTORS ON THE PURSUER'S SIDE

An invasion of comfortable enjoyment in terms of disturbance or inconvenience is less likely to lead to a reparation claim than actual physical harm. In such cases interdict will normally be the remedy sought. Reparation for personal injury is not excluded where it is incidental to nuisance. An example is the case of *Shanlin v Collins* where a woman suffered mental harm as a result of the barking of a neighbour's dogs. Physical harm may be to plants, crops, shrubs or trees, not just buildings or structures. Equally there may be harm to movable goods, as in *Ireland v Smith* in which the contents of a larder were destroyed by dust from a neighbour's chickens. Prospective harm may be interdicted, as in *Fleming v Hislop*, where the defenders were interdicted against setting light to bings.

The harm must be material. Disturbance must be substantial, inconvenience serious. Even in the case of physical damage it must be shown that the harm is material. There is a difference between the destruction of a field of crops and withered leaves on particularly sensitive shrubs. In determining materiality it is relevant to consider the degree and duration of the invasion. Noise disturbance is not simply a matter of volume, but there may be an element of quality. Thus, noise may be more than reasonably tolerable where persons are subjected in their homes to the sound of animals being dispatched in a slaughterhouse, as in *Kelt v Lindsay*, whereas louder noises from other sources might not possess the same disturbing qualities. People can reasonably be expected to put up with temporary disturbances, such as those caused by road works. Equally, time is relevant, so bell ringing might be tolerable during the day but a different matter in the middle of the night. A tourist season, such as the Edinburgh Festival, may increase the level of disturbance that must be tolerated.

There is not much discussion in the case law on the social value of the use invaded. It is clear, however, that lawful uses, whether residential, industrial, commercial or recreational, can be protected.

The relation between the use of land invaded and the character of the locality is less relevant to physical harm than it is to comfortable enjoyment. This does not mean that it is of no relevance and it has been argued that the strict division found between the types of harm in the English case of *St*

Helens Smelting Co v Tipping does not apply in Scotland. In *Watt v Jamieson* Lord Cooper considered that locality was generally relevant in nuisance and *Watt* involved physical harm. In *Maguire v Charles McNeil Ltd* the Archbishop of Glasgow, among other pursuers, failed to interdict the use of drop hammers in a forge. He was resident in a district in which there was much heavy industry. Nevertheless, even in such circumstances it is clear that a material increase in existing disturbance may give rise to a successful action in nuisance.

The sensitivity to harm of the pursuer or the pursuer's property is a relevant consideration in balancing the parties' interests. The *de minimis* rule operates. In nuisance this has been expressed as *lex non favet delicatorum votis*, "the law does not consider the wishes of the fastidious". Particularly sensitive land uses or extraordinarily sensitive persons may not be protected against disturbance that the reasonable occupier would be able to tolerate. However, in the context of personal injury, the thin skull rule in *McKillen v Barclay Curle* was followed to allow reparation for nervous debility in *Shanlin v Collins*. In *Armistead v Bowerman* the pursuer failed to obtain damages when fry were destroyed in a fish hatchery as a result of the defender's logging operations. In such sensitive circumstances there is a greater onus on the victim to implement prophylactic measures.

If one can easily protect oneself from disturbance by adopting simple remedial measures, such as shutting windows or airing rooms, then it is unlikely that there will be a finding of nuisance. On the other hand, one is not expected to remain indoors in order to avoid noise or smoke disturbance in the garden. It is not the case that there will be no finding of nuisance where it is simpler and cheaper for the victim to adopt remedial measures than it is for the defender to abate.

RELEVANT FACTORS ON THE DEFENDER'S SIDE

As noted, the reasonableness of the defender's use of land is not a complete defence, but a factor that may be weighed in the balance. Socially useful conduct, such as that which generates employment is more likely to be regarded as reasonable, compared with unlawful, malicious or indecent activities. Temporary interferences, such as road works, must be borne, but duration may prove relevant, as in *The Globe v North of Scotland Water Authority*. In this case the pursuers were allowed a proof before answer where road works scheduled to last six weeks continued over nine months. Mud on the pavement from the operation was alleged to have discouraged custom resulting in a reduction in takings in a pub.

The social utility of an activity cannot override the interest of the victim in their use of land. This is demonstrated in *Ben Nevis Distillery (Fort William) Ltd v The North British Aluminium Co Ltd*. The operation which the pursuers sought to have interdicted involved 72 per cent of UK aluminium production and a significant number of jobs. In this case interdict was awarded, but its operation was suspended to allow the defenders to implement remedial measures. A similar result was achieved in *Webster v Lord Advocate*, in which a resident found the noise from preparations for the Edinburgh Tattoo intolerable.

It must be noted that interdicts may be drawn up in a way that allows for the continuation of an activity, but not in such a way as to give rise to nuisance. In this way interdict can be used to regulate activities and effect abatement of nuisance. It must also be noted that, while the Court of Session has power to suspend an interdict, this power is exercised where either, in the words of Lord McLaren in *Clippens Oil Co v Edinburgh & District Water Trustees*:

> "[T]he granting of immediate interdict would be attended with consequences to the rights of the respondents as injurious, or possibly more so, than the wrong that was complained of or…because the effect of an immediate interdict would be to cause some great and immediate public inconvenience."

Before the power to suspend interdict is exercised, it is necessary first to reach a finding on the facts (*Ben Nevis Distillery*).

The less suitable to the character of the locality the more likely an operation is to be held to amount to nuisance. Reference may be made to the Local Development Plan whereby land is designated for residential, industrial or recreational purposes, but this will not necessarily be conclusive since smoke or noise may travel from an industrial zone to a residential one. The correct application of the planning process does not preclude a finding of nuisance.

Where harm is found to be more than reasonably tolerable, evidence of care taken will not preclude a finding of nuisance, however, it may go some way to establishing the defender's case. Abatement may be required by the terms of interdict. Equally, pronouncement of final interdict may be deferred to allow remedial measures to take place.

DEFENCES

Defences must be distinguished from factors taken into account in the process of applying the *plus quam tolerabile* test. A defence, if established, will override a finding of nuisance.

Statutory authority for the operation complained of may provide a defence, but only where nuisance is the inevitable outcome of the operation, irrespective of measures that may be taken to effect abatement. The defender may be called upon to show that all care has been taken, but nuisance is the inevitable outcome.

Acquiescence affords a defence equivalent to *volenti non fit injuria* in other areas of delict. *Volenti* does not appear to apply since the rule is that it is no defence that the complainer came to the nuisance. See, for example, *Fleming v Hislop* and *Webster v Lord Advocate*.

For acquiescence to succeed as a defence it is necessary to show that the pursuer had full knowledge of and consented, not merely to the activity complained of, but also to the harm or disturbance. This consent must be shown by something more positive than silence or a failure to object, although tolerance of the situation over a long period of time will point towards acquiescence. Acquiescence will not preclude an action where there is a material increase in the level of disturbance or harm.

Contributory fault has no role to play in nuisance. The Law Reform (Contributory Negligence) Act 1945 does not apply. Any role played by the pursuer, for example a failure to take simple remedial measures may be taken into account in balancing the interests of the parties.

It is not possible to acquire a prescriptive right to create a nuisance. On the other hand the right to object to nuisance may be lost after 20 years under s.8 of the Prescription and Limitation (Scotland) Act 1973. The right to seek reparation will also be lost after 20 years by virtue of s.8. The prescriptive period does not begin to run from the start of the offensive operation, but from the point at which it amounts to nuisance.

STATUTORY NUISANCE

It is an unusual feature that common law and statutory nuisance are seldom treated together. There are a large number of provisions dotted around statute law that deal with nuisance. There is a body of provisions to be found in the Environmental Protection Act 1990. The term "statutory nuisance" is normally taken to refer to this particular body of law. These provisions ultimately derive from the Public Health (Scotland) Act of 1867 though they have been through various incarnations since, most recent amendments being made by the Public Health (Scotland) Act 2008. While it has been the case, at least since *R v White and Ward*, that common law nuisance is not primarily concerned with health, but with amenity and the comfortable enjoyment of property, the statutory measures arose explicitly from the inability of the common law and earlier statutes to deal effectively with sanitation and matters of public health. These concerns were prompted especially by a number of cholera epidemics during the nineteenth century. While authors have, with varying degrees of success, sought to provide an integrated treatment of common law and statutory nuisance, it is probably true to say that the prevalent view is that statutory nuisance belongs in public rather than private law. Common law and statutory nuisance do, however, relate to one another and drawing a strict line between them is hardly satisfactory so statutory nuisance is included here albeit the treatment is very brief.

The current list of statutory nuisances under the EPA is provided below. It will be seen that many of the situations that once gave rise to common law nuisance actions now fall to be regulated under this provision. This does not in any sense limit the range of the common law but, because in statutory nuisance the law is mobilised by the local authority, it will often prove more practicable to complain to the authority rather than to initiate common law proceedings oneself. It is suggested that the implementation of public health measures along with the institution of effective planning regimes have had the effect of reducing the number of amenity nuisance claims raised at common law. By this it is meant that people are less likely now to raise civil actions seeking interdict in respect of water pollution, smoke, noise, heat or vibration than they were in the early nineteenth century. If the actions grounded in nuisance raised since the start of the twentieth century are examined it looks almost as if common law nuisance has survived by shifting ground to find a new niche for itself. Modern nuisance litigation has become less concerned with amenity and more focussed on tangible physical damage, especially when caused by flooding and withdrawal of support. It has been suggested in connection with English private nuisance that its role in the modern context is residual, it provides a safety net in circumstances where statutory authorities fail to act. The same suggestion might aptly be made for nuisance in the common law of Scotland.

Section 79(1) of the Environmental Protection Act 1990 lists statutory nuisances as follows:

(a) any premises in such a state as to be prejudicial to health or a nuisance;
(b) smoke emitted from premises so as to be prejudicial to health or a nuisance;
(c) fumes or gases emitted from premises so as to be prejudicial to health or a nuisance;
(d) any dust, steam, smell or other effluvia arising on industrial trade or business premises so as to be prejudicial to health or a nuisance;
(e) any accumulation or deposit which is prejudicial to health or a nuisance;
(ea) any water covering land or land covered with water which is in such a state as to be prejudicial to health or a nuisance;
(f) any animal kept in such a place or manner as to be prejudicial to health or a nuisance;
(faa) any insects emanating from premises and being prejudicial to health or a nuisance;
(fba) artificial light emitted from:
    (i) premises;
    (ii) any stationary object,
    so as to be prejudicial to health or a nuisance;
(g) noise emitted from premises so as to be prejudicial to health or a nuisance;
(ga) noise that is prejudicial to health or a nuisance and is emitted from or caused by a vehicle, machinery or equipment in a street or in Scotland, road;
(h) any other matter declared by any enactment to be a statutory nuisance.

The law is enforced by local authorities. Each local authority is under a duty to detect statutory nuisances and, where complaints are brought, to take reasonable steps to investigate. Where statutory nuisance is found, the authority is obliged under s.80 to issue a notice to ensure that the nuisance is abated. Those on whom the abatement notice is served have a right of appeal to the sheriff court. Contravention of an abatement notice constitutes a criminal offence (s.80(4)). Liability to conviction may be discharged on payment of a fixed penalty (s.80 (4A)).

Accordingly, if one suffers discomfort or inconvenience from some source regulated by the Environmental Protection Act, it is more simple to complain to the local authority than to embark on the process of seeking interdict through the civil courts. However, the aggrieved citizen is not entirely dependent upon the response of the authority. Section 82 allows for direct application to the sheriff court by individuals.

As noted, there are a large number of provisions dotted around statute law which deal with nuisance. In this brief treatment one final example will suffice. Imagine you live in a tenement flat and your neighbour practises the electric guitar throughout the night at full volume. This could be the subject of interdict. The most straightforward way of dealing with the problem, however, is usually to call the police, on the basis that your neighbour is giving reasonable cause for annoyance. If your neighbour fails to desist, having been ordered to do so by a constable in uniform, they will have committed an offence under s.54(1) of the Civil Government (Scotland) Act 1982. The drawback to this course of procedure is that it may not always be possible to get police to respond to such a call. Failing police action a complaint to the local authority would be in order. The circumstances suggest a statutory nuisance under EPA s.79(1)(g). Local authorities do not always act. In such a case it may prove necessary to seek declarator and interdict in the local sheriff court.

9. NOMINATE DELICTS

INTRODUCTION

The delicts considered in this chapter may be termed nominate delicts, because they have names. Admittedly defamation and nuisance are also nominate delicts, but these merit separate treatment in their own chapters. In *Micosta v Shetlands Islands Council* Lord Ross made the following observation:

> "There is no such thing as an exhaustive list of named delicts in the law of Scotland. If the conduct complained of appears to be wrongful, the Law of Scotland will afford a remedy even if there has not been any previous instance of a remedy being given in similar circumstances...The decision to recognise a particular interest, and consequently to grant a remedy for its infringement, is a question of social policy, and the list recognised has grown over the years."

This is a point of great significance for the development of the law in the modern context, especially when contrasted with the position in England. English law operates with recognised torts and, consequently, has much difficulty in allowing redress in circumstances that do not fit squarely within the boundaries of established wrongs. Two examples will serve to illustrate the point. In *Khorasandjian v Bush* the Court of Appeal granted an injunction in respect of nuisance to a girl who was greatly troubled by persistent, unwanted phone calls from an ex-boyfriend. This was a majority decision influenced strongly by Canadian authority and was problematic in terms of private nuisance, because the girl had no proprietary interest in the house in which she received the calls. English private nuisance is essentially a tort against land and originally the assize of nuisance was open only to freeholders. This decision was not allowed to stand for long. *Khorasandjian* was overruled by the House of Lords in *Hunter v Canary Wharf* and English rules on title to sue in nuisance restored. In the interim, Parliament had enacted the Protection From Harassment Act and so legal redress is now available to persons who are being stalked or harassed. This protection, however, is on a statutory basis, the common law having proved somewhat inflexible.

A further example is provided by the issue of privacy. Privacy is a human right within the scope of Art.8 of the European Convention on Human Rights and there is accordingly pressure on jurisdictions to recognise it as a reparable interest. While the courts in Scotland have yet to be presented with the opportunity to determine an approach, English law has stopped short of recognising breach of privacy as a tort, diverting "privacy" cases into breach of confidence.

The relative fluidity of the Scots approach can be seen in cases such as *Henderson v Chief Constable of Fife Police*, in which striking laboratory workers at the Victoria Hospital in Kirkcaldy were taken into police custody. One male pursuer recovered damages because he was unjustifiably handcuffed. A female pursuer recovered because she was required to remove her bra. It is not unusual for persons admitted to police cells to be asked to hand over ties or shoelaces in order to prevent them from hanging themselves. However, in this instance, where the pursuer was co-operative and there was no suggestion that she would seek to harm herself, it was held that the removal of her bra constituted an unjustifiable infringement of her liberty. This may be contrasted with the English case of *Wainwright v Home Office*, in which the court was unable to award damages in respect of distress and humiliation caused by an improperly conducted strip search on a mother and son, when visiting another son in prison, because no known tort had occurred. The claimants were ultimately awarded damages at the European Court of Human Rights (*Wainwright v UK*) for breach of Art.13. They had not had available to them a means for obtaining redress for interference with their rights under Art.8.

The Roman *actio injuriarum* has been significant in developing the open nature of delictual liability, especially in terms of the recognition of affront as sufficient to constitute actionable loss. This view has been affirmed recently in the case of *Stevens v Yorkhill NHS Trust*, in which the pursuer was granted damages following the unauthorised removal and retention of her deceased child's brain during *post mortem* examination. It was held in the Outer House that this was an actionable wrong known to Scots common law and based on the *actio injuriarum*. In Rome the *actio injuriarum* provided remedies in respect of a broad range of affronts and insults, covering not only verbal injury but also such matters as physical assault, affronts to a woman's modesty including stalking and making improper suggestions, and interfering with freedom of movement in public places. It has been argued that the *actio injuriarum* could serve as a model for future development more generally, but this is regarded in some quarters with scepticism. Nevertheless, the point serves as fuel for healthy academic debate.

Some nominate delicts such as seduction, entrapment and enticement have dropped out of practical use and others, such as assythment, have been abolished by statute. Some nominate delicts have rules of liability or defences peculiar to themselves. The important points to note are that a remedy is available wherever a reparable interest has been wrongfully invaded, that the recognition of new reparable interests is a matter of policy and that Scots law is relatively open to new sorts of claim.

The treatment of nominate delicts that follows is necessarily selective and brief.

DELICTS AGAINST THE PERSON

Assault
Assault is both a crime and a civil wrong. Where the perpetrator has been convicted in the criminal courts, a compensation order in favour of the victim may be made in terms of the Criminal Injuries Compensation scheme. Occasionally, where prosecution is not successful, a civil action may be pursued. Even though the *mens rea* necessary for criminal conviction is lacking, a civil case may yet succeed since liability is established on the balance of probabilities. This is a lesser standard than that applied in the criminal courts where the case must be proved beyond reasonable doubt. Of course, raising a civil action in assault is in no sense dependent upon any criminal proceedings.

While it is clear that reparation can be sought in respect of invasions of bodily integrity the essence of this delict is not so much physical harm as insult or affront to dignity. The Scots approach here derives from the *actio injuriarum*. Liability in assault is based on intention. Accidentally inflicted injuries are not actionable in assault. It is important to note that it is not necessary to establish the intention to harm the victim, only that the harmful act was intentional in the sense of being deliberately carried out. In delictual liability motive is, with very few exceptions, irrelevant. This is made abundantly clear by the case of *Reid v Mitchell* in which a farm worker fell from a hay cart as a result of "larking about" by his fellow workers. He recovered damages, notwithstanding the absence of any specific desire to cause him injury.

Physical injury or even contact is not a necessary requirement for liability. In *Cock v Neville* a farmer was awarded a small sum of damages in respect of threats and abuse he had received from army officers trespassing on his land. In 1834, in *Tullis v Glenday* the sum of £40 in damages was awarded to the pursuer who alleged the defender had spat in his face. The sum claimed was £500! In *Ewing v Earl of Mar* it was held to amount to assault to ride a horse at a pedestrian, causing danger and alarm, and it was also insulting and an assault to spit at a person whether or not the spit landed on the victim.

To be actionable an assault must have been without the consent of the victim, so complaints of assault are inapplicable, for example, in contact sports such as boxing or rugby where the invasion of physical integrity is part and parcel of the game. However, this limitation only applies so long as the rules of the game are adhered to. A boxer might be able to recover in respect of a below-the-belt injury, similarly a hooker who has had his ear bitten off by an opposing prop forward would have an action in delict for assault.

The action may be defended if it can be shown that the defender acted in self-defence or if the assault was the result of an unavoidable accident. As in the criminal law, provocation does not provide a defence. Where established, provocation may operate as a mitigating factor to reduce any sum awarded in damages.

Wrongful detention

The interest protected here is the liberty of the person. Nobody can be unlawfully detained against their will. The classic case of damages in respect of wrongful detention is *Mackenzie v Cluny Hill Hydropathic Company* in which a female guest was detained by the hotel manager in his office for some 15 minutes. The pursuer was expected to apologise to two other guests whom she was alleged to have slighted. The pursuer successfully recovered damages in respect of the infringement of her liberty and affront.

Such instances of hotel managers taking upon themselves the role of a headteacher are thankfully rare. Complaints of wrongful detention are more likely to arise in connection with police activities. Scope for a successful case of wrongful arrest is limited. So long as police officers act within the law no claim in delict should arise. Where arrest is carried out without warrant, this may be justified on grounds of reasonable suspicion.

A suspected shoplifter may be detained for a reasonable time until the police arrive. However, following *Pringle v Bremner & Stirling*, in order to evade liability, suspicions must be reasonably held.

Liberty, moreover, is a human right protected by art.5 of the European Convention on Human Rights. Thus deprivation of liberty by those acting on behalf of the state is actionable, but it is argued, following *Storck v Germany*, that there is a positive obligation on states to prevent the deprivation of liberty by private actors (AIL Campbell, "Positive Obligations under the ECHR: Deprivation of Liberty by Private Actors" (2006) 10 Edin. L.R. 399–412).

Harassment

Contravention of lawburrows is an old delict that is technically still competent. Where an individual anticipates harassment, violence or molestation, the delinquent may be called upon to lodge a sum of money known as caution with the court. In the event that lawburrows is contravened — that is, the cautioner harasses or molests the petitioner — the caution is forfeit. Lawburrows is a surviving relic of the period when there was no effective means of criminal law enforcement and the law of delict played a quasi-criminal role in keeping the peace. The best known twentieth century case is *Liddle v Morton*. The most recent example is *Duff v Strang*. *Duff v Strang* demonstrates that appeals against the determinations of a sheriff lie only in the civil courts. It is incompetent to appeal to the High Court of Justiciary. The case suggests that a fairly broad view may be taken of the behaviour that may be subject to lawburrows, the petitioner complained of alleged defamatory statements made by police officers. His action failed, not because of the nature of the molestation, but because he did not establish apprehension of future occurrences.

Nowadays a person who fears harassment is much more likely to invoke the Protection from Harassment Act 1997. Sections 8 and 9 apply in Scotland.

The victim may raise an action of harassment. The remedies available are interdict, interim interdict, non-harassment orders and damages. Interdict and non-harassment orders are mutually exclusive. A non-harassment order is viewed as being more serious and the courts will not make such an award where an interdict would be sufficient. This may be seen in *McGuire v Kidston*. Damages are recoverable both in respect of anxiety and any financial loss. For any remedy it must be established that there has been harassment amounting to a course of conduct, there must have been harassment on at least two occasions. Harassment is not statutorily defined. It must also be established that the defender's conduct was intended to amount to harassment, or viewed objectively, may reasonably be interpreted in that way. Breach of a non-harassment order is a criminal offence. Defences to an action of harassment are that the conduct was authorised by law; the conduct was pursued for the purposes of preventing or detecting crime; or the conduct was reasonable in the circumstances.

While the Act was, to some extent, motivated as a legal response to stalking, it may be noted that in Scots law there are two new criminal offences that are relevant in harassment. These are the offence of threatening or abusive behaviour under s.38 of the Criminal Justice and Licensing (Scotland) Act 2010 and the offence of stalking under s.39 of the same Act.

Under the common law it was possible for a person to conduct a campaign of harassment against a fellow employee without a sufficient connection between employment and the acts being established for vicarious liability to arise. This was the result in *Ward v Scotrail Railways Ltd*. While it remains the case that a course of conduct amounting to harassment must be sufficiently connected to employment for vicarious liability on the part of the employer to arise, employers may now be held vicariously liable where employees are harassed at work within the meaning of s.8 of the Protection From Harassment Act 1997. This follows from the ruling of the Court of Appeal in *Majrowski v Guy's and St Thomas' NHS Trust*, albeit that case proceeded on provisions of the Act which do not apply in Scotland.

Racial abuse within the workplace also gives rise to vicarious liability. The Race Relations Act 1976 states:

> "Anything done by a person in the course of his employment shall be treated for the purposes of this Act (except as regards offences thereunder) as done by his employer as well as him, whether or not it was done with the employer's knowledge or approval..." (s.32(1))

In *Jones v Tower Boot Co Ltd* Raymondo Jones sought damages in respect of racial abuse carried out by two fellow employees. The industrial tribunal held the employer vicariously liable by virtue of s.32. This decision was reversed by the Employment Appeal Tribunal on the basis that the abusers could not be described as acting in the course of their employment. Racial abuse was not an unauthorised mode of working, it was a series of independent acts. The House of Lords, in seeking to give effect to the intention of Parliament to eliminate racial discrimination, held the employer liable. The words "in the course of his employment" were to be given their ordinary, everyday meaning and not construed in accordance with common law rules on vicarious liability. Accordingly, where an employee is subjected to racial abuse by fellow employees, the employer will be vicariously liable under statute and common law rules on establishing vicarious liability will not apply.

Breach of confidence/ Misuse of private information

It is a delict to publish or otherwise disseminate information provided in confidence, or information gained from a relationship of confidence such as between banker and client, solicitor and client or doctor and patient. The obligation arises wherever there is a relationship of confidence, irrespective of whether there is a contractual relationship, and is not restricted to the commercial sphere. The *locus classicus* is *Prince Albert v Strange*. Copperplates made by Prince Albert and Queen Victoria were entrusted to a workman. He made impressions and these were sold to a third party. Prince Albert succeeded in gaining an injunction against further publication and a court order requiring remaining copies to be destroyed. *Ash v McKennitt* and *Associated Newspapers Ltd v HRH The Prince of Wales* are recent examples of cases arising from breaches of relationships of trust.

The United Kingdom is obliged to give protection to "private and family life" under Art.8 of the European Convention on Human Rights as enacted in the Human Rights Act 1998. The law of breach of confidence has been adapted to provide redress. The most significant change made to the old law on confidentiality is that the need for a relationship of confidence has been dispensed with. This was established by the House of Lords in *Campbell v MGN*. The model Naomi Campbell claimed breach of her right to privacy when the *Mirror* published details of her drug rehabilitation treatment along with a covertly taken photograph of her leaving a group therapy session. The defendant had argued that the publication was justified in the public interest since Ms Campbell had misled the public by declaring that she did not take drugs. While it was accepted in the House of Lords that it was legitimate to establish that Ms Campbell had lied to the public, the information published was held by a majority to be confidential and damages were awarded. This decision was aided by the relation of the treatment to the mental and physical health of the claimant, meaning that a tenuous parallel could be drawn with medical records which are in all cases confidential. Since *Campbell*, remedies have been available against the dissemination of information in respect of which there is a reasonable expectation of privacy. It has been held that there is an expectation of privacy in relation to sexual activities between adults carried out in private, even when the activities are "unconventional" (*Mosely v News Group Newspapers Ltd*). The publication of photographs may also give rise to remedies, the most famous instance is *Von Hanover v Germany*. In *Murray v Express Newspapers plc* it was held that privacy rights were breached when a photograph of the son of JK Rowling, taken without permission, was published.

While an obligation of confidence can be inferred from a relationship or, as in *Campbell* and *Mosely*, from the nature of the information itself, the obligation can also be imposed, that is information can be made confidential by agreement. In this way, trade secrets may be protected by an obligation of confidentiality inserted in a contract of employment in the form of a restrictive covenant. Such terms are enforceable so long as they are drawn no wider than necessary to protect the legitimate business interests of the party relying on them. The case of *Douglas v Hello!* shows the imposition of an obligation of confidentiality on wedding photographs by contractual means. The Douglases granted exclusive rights to publish their wedding photographs to *OK!* magazine. Under the terms of the contract the happy couple were to take all reasonable steps to restrict access to their wedding to prevent other media from obtaining pictures. A freelance photographer infiltrated proceedings and took pictures which *Hello!* magazine then published. In the House of Lords it was held by a majority that the pictures were confidential and of commercial value and that there was no policy reason why *OK!* should not be able to protect the rights they had acquired under contract against *Hello!* Damages of over £1 million were awarded.

A new phenomenon that has emerged in the English Courts from privacy actions is the super-injunction. A super-injunction contains an express prohibition on those on whom it is served against revealing the fact that an injunction has been granted. Examples of applications for super-injunctions may be found in *Terry (Formerly LNS) v Persons Unknown* and in the *Trafigura* litigation (*(1) RJW (2) SJW v Guardian News and Media Ltd (2) the Person or Persons Unknown*). In the former a professional footballer sought to prevent the dissemination of truthful information regarding his sexual adventures, in the latter an oil company sought to prevent dissemination of information in a privately commissioned report into the dumping of toxic waste off the Ivory Coast. Had either of these applications been ultimately successful then it would not have been possible to write about them here. While the courts have a difficult job in balancing the right to private and family life with the Art.10 right to freedom of expression, super-injunctions do raise serious concerns that those sufficiently rich to be able to afford the litigation will use the law to stifle any form of adverse criticism. Increasingly, there are calls for legislation in this area.

DELICTS AGAINST PROPERTY

Trespass and related delicts

There is a myth that there is no such thing as trespass in Scots law. This is quite untrue. The point is that, in contrast to England, no damages are available for a bare trespass. There must be actual damage before there can be reparation.

Historically, the idea of exclusive rights of possession of land did not gain ground until around the end of the eighteenth century, by which time much land had been enclosed and land registration was sufficiently reliable. There was very little litigation prior to the nineteenth century and what little there was arose primarily from straying domestic animals and persons in pursuit of game. Stair did not consider trespass; Bell was the first institutional writer to accord it any detailed treatment.

Trespass is concerned with temporary and unjustifiable intrusions onto heritable property. The interest protected is the right to exclusive use and possession. Permanent physical intrusions, such as walls, overhanging eaves or even branches are not trespass, but encroachment (see, for example, *Halkerston v Wedderburn*). As Guthrie-Smith wrote in 1864, "[a]n owner of real property must carefully confine himself and his operations within his own boundary. His erections must not project on his neighbour's ground, nor his trees overhang the intervening wall." Squatting is not trespass but intrusion. Intrusion operates where the owner is not in possession at the time. Where the owner is ejected from the property this is yet another delict, ejection.

Heritable property is owned *a coelo usque ad centrum*, that is "from the sky to the centre of the earth", so air space above the property is protected against trespass and encroachment. However, trespass may not be mobilised against over-flying aircraft by virtue of the Civil Aviation Act 1982 s.2. Trespass on moveable property that may be occupied, such as ships or oil rigs, is actionable (see *Phestos Shipping Co Ltd v Kurmiawan* and *Shell UK Ltd v McGillivray*).

While damages are available in respect of tangible harm done, for example, to crops, the primary remedy against trespass is interdict. Interdict is a discretionary remedy and will only be awarded in circumstances that are deemed appropriate. Interdict may be refused, for example, because of the triviality of the invasion complained of. The most famous case is *Winans v MacRae* in which the owner of 200,000 acres of deer forest was refused interdict to prevent a pet lamb from straying onto his land.

For an award of interdict there must be reasonable apprehension that future trespass will occur (see, for example, *Hay's Trustees v Young*). Interdict is personal and is only effective against persons named on the petition. An interdict against one person will not be effective against another who is not named. Interdict may be effective in cases of sit-ins in industrial disputes. For example, in *Caterpillar (UK) Ltd* interdict was granted against 808 named individuals. In other circumstances it may be impossible to identify the relevant individuals (see, for example, *Stirling Crawfurd v Clyde Navigation Trustees*). It has been observed that interdict in trespass is only truly effective against persistent identifiable individuals.

While proprietors can take precautionary measures to protect their privacy, it is highly doubtful whether reasonable force can be used to eject trespassers. While Bell considered that the use of man traps was legitimate (para.961) this is clearly not the case in the modern law in which a duty of care is owed to trespassers under the Occupiers' Liability (Scotland) Act. Cases that have been founded upon to support a right to reasonable use of force (*Bell v Shand*; *Aitchison v Thorburn* and *Wood v North British Railway*) do not support the use of force except where, as in *Wood*, it is explicitly sanctioned by statute. The use of force is likely to give rise to liability in assault.

The most significant development in the law has been the coming into force of Statutory Access Rights under the Land Reform (Scotland) Act 2003. This Act creates extensive statutory rights to enter land belonging to others. It also imposes a regulatory regime which is likely to interact with common law remedies against trespass.

Section 1 provides everybody with two distinct rights. One is the right to be on land for specified purposes of recreation, educational activities or commercial enterprises. The other is the right to cross land. These rights only exist to the extent that they are exercised responsibly (s.2). Under s.28 the existence and extent of access rights and questions of responsibility may be determined by the sheriff court on summary application.

Land excepted from statutory access rights is defined in ss.6 and 7. For example, access rights may not be exercised in buildings or in the curtilage of buildings, although curtilage is undefined. Equally land around houses sufficient to provide the occupants with a reasonable measure of privacy is excluded. There is a right to cross golf courses, but the greens are excluded from access rights under s.7(7)(b).

Certain activities are specifically excluded under s.9. Local Authorities have the power to regulate access under ss.11–27. The responsibilities of landowners and persons exercising access rights are set out in the Access Code drawn up by Scottish Natural Heritage (*www.outdooraccess-scotland.com* [accessed May 11, 2011]). This code does not have the force of law, but has evidentiary value. Responsible access is summarised in the code in the following terms: "take responsibility for your own actions; respect people's privacy and peace of mind; help land managers and others to work safely and effectively; care for your environment; keep your dog under proper control; and take extra care if you are organising an event or running a business".

The code also provides a long list of activities that are deemed "recreational" within the meaning of the Act. These include watching wildlife, sightseeing, painting and photography and family and social activities such as dog walking, picnics and sledging. Also listed are active pursuits such as climbing, caving, canoeing and wild camping. It has been observed that the code does not note whether sex is a recreational purpose within the meaning of the Act. Educational purposes under the Act would include visiting historic sights and geology field trips. Relevant commercial activities include mountain guiding or survival courses undertaken for profit, but not extractive industry!

There is a slowly growing body of case law on the Act. *Gloag v Perth & Kinross District Council* concerned the extent of land around a private dwelling that could legitimately be excluded from access rights. Under s.6(1)(b)(iv) a sufficient area of land may be excluded to allow a reasonable degree of privacy. The view was taken that what is sufficient is a function of the requirements of a reasonable person living in that type of house. There is some suggestion that persons living in big houses will be entitled to a greater area from which access can be excluded. By contrast the pursuers in *Forbes v Fife Council* were unable to have a path behind their back gardens which was common property between them, declared excluded from access rights under s.28. In *Aviemore Highland Resort Ltd v Cairngorms National Park Authority* it was held incompetent to serve a s.14 notice to remove an obstruction to access which had been in place before the Act came into force. In *Tuley v Highland Council* proprietors were held to be acting reasonably in restricting equestrian access in order to preserve the state of the path for pedestrian access.

Clearly rights may now be exercised over much land where previously people could have been excluded by interdict. It must be noted that the exclusions are complicated and the question over whether rights are exercised responsibly may give rise to difficulty. It may be thought that interdict will remain a competent remedy where persons enter land that is unambiguously excluded or where behaviour is clearly not responsible under the Act. Where either or both of these points are arguable then it remains to be seen whether interdicts will be granted in circumstances where petitioners have not first sought a declaratory ruling under s.28. Certainly in the past courts have refused interdict in circumstances where alternative remedial measures have not been implemented (see, for example, *Paterson v McPherson* and *Campbell v Mackay*). It is thought that the statutory mechanisms for regulating access may have to be exhausted before the common law remedy is granted.

Certain forms of trespass are criminal acts. For example, under the Trespass (Scotland) Act 1868 s.3(1) camping on land without permission or lighting a fire is punishable. However, under Sch.2 of the Land Reform Act these no longer amount to offences where statutory access rights are exercised. Section 61 of the Criminal Justice and Public Order Act 1994 creates an offence where a common purpose has been formed to reside on land or where threatening, abusive or insulting behaviour has been used towards the occupier, his family or agents. This is collective trespass. It operates with a minimum of two trespassers and the necessary first step is for the occupier to take reasonable steps to ask the trespassers to leave. The police have powers to remove collective trespassers. Returning to the land within three months or a failure to remove when required to do so is an offence.

In cases of a single trespasser, damage to land may amount to vandalism. Threatening, abusive or insulting behaviour is a breach of the peace. Specific forms of damage may amount to offences under other statutes, such as the Wildlife and Countryside Act 1981 or the Environmental Protection Act 1990. Driving a vehicle off road without permission is specifically excluded from statutory access rights under s.9(f) and is an offence under s.34 of the Road Traffic Act 1988.

The most important common law defence to trespass is justification. By definition, a trespass is an unjustifiable intrusion so where there is justification there is no trespass. It is accepted, for instance, that there is no trespass where land is entered to apprehend a criminal or to fight a fire. Furthermore, there are many instances in which entering land is authorised by statute. Acquiescence also provides a defence. Consent to enter land may be express or implied, but consent, once given, can always be withdrawn (see, for example, *Steuart v Stephen* and *Love-Lee v Cameron of Locheil*).

Use of land in aemulationem vicini
This delict is broadly similar to nuisance although it pre-dates nuisance in Scots law considerably. It means spiteful or malicious use of land with the intention of causing harm to a neighbour. The relevant category of *culpa* is malice. Accordingly, the motive of the defender is relevant.

In order for malice to be inferred it must be clear that the predominant purpose of the activity complained of was to harm or annoy. Therefore if the defender can establish that the offensive act was conducted for their own convenience or benefit and that harm to the pursuer was merely consequential, then an action *in aemulationem* will be defeated (see, for example, *Dewar v Fraser*). In such circumstances a claim in nuisance would be more appropriate since nuisance does not require malice.

Examples of cases in which *aemulatio* was successfully pled include *Campbell v Muir* and *More v Boyle*. In the former, petitioner and respondent were neighbouring proprietors on opposite banks of the river Awe. The respondent moored his boat in the middle of the river and cast his rod in such a way as to prevent Sir Robert Usher, who had leased the fishing rights from the petitioner, from continuing to fish. Sir Robert had been fishing at that spot for five minutes before the arrival of Muir. The pool where the men were fishing was some 60 yards wide by 146 yards long. Therefore there was plenty of space for Muir to fish the pool without interfering with Sir Robert. The case *in aemulationem* was established.

In *More v Boyle* the defender severed a water connection in his back garden in order to "get his own back" on neighbours who had refused to pay for a repair on the water pipe. The case *in aemulationem* was held relevant.

Wrongful interference with moveable property

The law of delict in this area is somewhat obscure, particularly since the continuing relevance of the old delict of spuilzie is highly debatable. Bankton described spuilzie as "the violent seizing, or unlawful taking possession of goods from another, without his consent or order of law, for lucre's sake". Originally spuilzie provided a remedy against violent dispossession or theft under which the goods would be restored to their lawful possessor. Spuilzie came also to deal with technical wrongs such as wrongfully withholding goods, for example, under a poinding without judicial warrant. Although originating as early as 1318, litigation in spuilzie was at a peak from the fifteenth to the seventeenth centuries.

Twentieth century attempts to revive spuilzie have contributed more confusion than clarity to the law. Examples of cases in which spuilzie has been discussed include: *FC Finance Ltd v Brown & Son*; *Mercantile Credit Company Ltd v Townsley*; *Harris v Abbey National plc*; and *Gemmell v Bank of Scotland*.

The Scottish Law Commission (Memo. 31, 1976) suggested that the action of spuilzie was in need of radical reform. They also stated that "the invocation of ancient remedies of uncertain scope is not necessarily the ideal solution for modern wrongs". Indeed, wrongful interference with moveable property can normally be dealt with by other means—by simple application of the principle of *culpa*, by negligence, by the law of property or by the principles of restitution.

FRAUD AND THE ECONOMIC DELICTS

Fraud

Erskine's definition of fraud is "a machination or contrivance to deceive". Fraud is established where an untrue statement or representation is made, or where the statement is believed to be untrue or where the person making the statement is recklessly indifferent whether it be true or false.

Fraud is an intentional delict. It is important to note that the restrictions on recovery of pure economic loss that apply in unintentional or negligent wrongdoing do not apply in intentional delicts. Of course, the form of loss to which fraud is most likely to give rise is economic.

Fraud arises most often in the context of misrepresentation inducing another party to contract. In such circumstances, fraud gives rise to both delictual and contractual remedies. For example, in the case of *Smith v Sim* the pursuer bought a pub in Montrose relying on turnover figures produced by the defender. The figures turned out to be fraudulent. Under the law of contract, Smith had the right to have the contract reduced. The fact that he chose not to exercise this right did not preclude him from recovering damages in delict in respect of fraud. As an alternative to damages, fraud may give rise to a right to restitution or recompense. For example, where a trader has fraudulently persuaded a person to part with a valuable painting it may be preferable for the victim to secure the return of the painting rather than to be compensated in damages.

Passing off

Broadly, passing off is an attempt by a trader to appropriate the goodwill of another trader. This occurs where the name or "get up" of a product is sufficiently similar to another product to amount to a misrepresentation that will confuse consumers. Loss is in the form of reduced sales or damaged reputation.

The essential elements of passing off are set out by Lord Diplock in *Erven Warnink BV v J Townend & Sons (Hull) Ltd (No.1)*. First, there is a misrepresentation. Secondly, the misrepresentation is made by a trader in the course of trade. Thirdly, the misrepresentation is made to prospective customers of his or ultimate consumers of goods and services provided by him. Fourthly, the misrepresentation is calculated to injure the business or goodwill of another trader. Fifthly, the misrepresentation has caused or probably will cause damage to the business or goodwill of the other trader.

The primary remedy in cases of passing off is interdict. Damages may also be available, although the process of quantifying loss may present problems. Statutory remedies exist where patents and copyrights are breached.

Inducing/procuring breach of contract

It is an actionable delict if a person induces another to breach a contract to which they are party. This is a relatively recent delict, recognised by Scots law in the case of *British Motor Trade Association v Gray*. Inducing a breach of contract is a wrong in itself. In order to be actionable the means used does not have to be unlawful. The innocent party to the contract can sue the party who induces the breach in delict. Of course, they may also sue the other party to the contract for breach. Before damages can be awarded, there must be loss. However, where breach has been induced courts will have little difficulty in inferring loss. Scottish courts require knowledge of the contract before a person can be held liable for inducing breach. The strong suggestion from the case of *Rossleigh Ltd v Leader Cars Ltd* is that actual knowledge of the existence of a contract is required, although the specific terms of the contract need not be known. The requirements for inducing a breach of contract were considered recently by the House of Lords in *Douglas v Hello!* The defender must know that he is causing a breach of contract and must intend to do so with knowledge of the consequences. A conscious decision not to enquire into the existence of facts can be treated as knowledge so where, in *Mainstream Properties Ltd v Young*, a financier had purchased development land in conjunction with two employees of the claimant who acted in breach of their contracts of employment, the financier was not liable because he had positively sought assurances from the employees and honestly believed that their joint venture would not breach their contracts. Knowing induction of a breach of contract as a means to an end demonstrates the necessary intent, even though motivated by the desire to secure an economic advantage rather than malice. On the other hand, a breach of contract which is neither a means to an end nor an end in itself, but is merely a foreseeable consequence of the defender's acts, does not give rise to liability. In *Douglas v Hello!* it was held that since there had been no breach of the contract between the Douglases and *OK!* there was no liability on this ground.

Inducing breach of contract deals with the situation where the delinquent is able to prevail on one party to the contract, perhaps by threats, perhaps by financial inducement, to breach. Procurement refers to the situation where the delinquent is able to engineer a breach of contract where the party is unwilling to breach. This can be done directly, for example, by vandalising machinery essential to performance of the contract, or indirectly, for example, by inducing a breach of contract on the part of a supplier. In contrast to inducing breach of contract, liability only arises in respect of procurement where unlawful means are used to procure the breach. For a recent example see *Global Resources Group v McKay*.

Wrongful interference with performance of contract/causing loss by unlawful means

It appeared at one time as though economic delicts, such as wrongful interference with contract and inducing breach, should be subsumed under a broader heading of wrongful interference with trade. More recently, in *OBG v Allan* the House of Lords appears to have re-asserted the distinction between inducing a breach of contract and causing loss by unlawful means by considering each as separate torts with their own requirements for liability. In this case the claimant sought damages after receivers had been appointed by an unsecured creditor. The receivers had terminated most of OBG's contracts. It was held by a majority, dismissing the claimant's appeal, that there had been no breach or non-performance of any contract, so there could be liability for neither inducing nor procuring breach of contract. Although the claimant had contended that the receivers had been wrongly appointed, it was held that, since they acted in good faith and had employed neither unlawful means nor intended loss to the claimants, there was no liability for causing loss by unlawful means. The requirement for liability of subjective intent to harm is confirmed in *Mainstream Properties Ltd v Young*. There was no liability on this ground in *Douglas v Hello!* as no unlawful means were employed.

Intimidation

This delict derives from the House of Lords case of *Rookes v Barnard (No.1)*. It arises where one party threatens a second with an unlawful act unless the second party causes economic harm to a third party. In *Rookes* three trade union officials threatened their employer, BOAC, with unlawful strike action unless Rookes' employment was terminated. Rookes succeeded in his case against the three officials.

Conspiracy

The delict of conspiracy requires a combination of parties acting together to cause economic harm to another party. If parties act together with the predominant motive of causing harm to another then liability in delict arises, whether or not the means used to inflict harm are unlawful. It may be noted that this is one of the rare instances in delictual liability in which motive is relevant.

Thus, while it is not an actionable delict for a business to attempt to drive another concern out of business, for example, by undercutting prices (see *Allen v Flood*), where two or more businesses or parties combine with the intention of causing economic harm then delictual liability arises. So a course of action that would not be delictual if carried out by a single party becomes delictual by virtue of conspiracy. Where the means used are lawful and the predominant motive behind any course of action is to benefit the participating parties and intention to cause harm to the pursuer is absent then no delict is committed. This follows from *Crofter Hand Woven Harris Tweed Co Ltd v Veitch*. The onus is on the pursuer to establish predominant motive to harm. The pursuer must also establish economic loss. Where the means used are unlawful, in the sense of being criminal, in breach of contract, in breach of statute or delictual, then the pursuer has to establish that the conspirators intended harm. They do not have to show that harm was the predominant motive for the acts.

---

10. REMEDIES

INTRODUCTION

Generally where loss is caused by a wrong, the law provides a remedy. Where the loss is quantifiable in money terms the remedy sought will usually be damages. However, depending on the circumstances, other remedies may be more appropriate.

The simplest remedy is self-help. Clearly the scope of self-help is limited. Its most clear application is in trespass. A landowner may construct a fence or dyke to keep other people or animals from straying onto their property. Trespassers may be asked to leave, but it is highly doubtful if force may be used to eject persons from premises or land. Trees or shrubs that encroach on land, for example, branches that overhang one's property, may be lopped or pruned with no right of recourse accruing to the owner.

A person who has been wronged may seek declarator. A declarator is given when a state of affairs amounting to a delict is found to exist. For example, a declarator may provide that a state of affairs amounts to a nuisance. Normally an action for declarator will be accompanied by a plea for damages or interdict since the award of declarator itself does not compel the defender to do anything, to refrain from doing anything or to pay anything. It is simply a statement of the legal position of the parties. A declarator may be useful to prevent the running of prescription and in nuisance it will defeat a later defence of acquiescence.

The principal remedies are interdict and damages. These are both complicated and entire books have been devoted to consideration of each. The following text is an outline guide to the essential points only.

INTERDICT

The essence of interdict is that prevention is better than cure. Interdict is sought to prevent an anticipated wrong or to put an end to a continuing wrong. An interdict restrains the activities of the party against whom it is awarded. In short, it forbids the party interdicted from conducting the activity specified. If the terms of the interdict are breached, the party in breach will be liable to a fine or imprisonment. The party seeking the interdict is the petitioner. The party against whom the interdict is sought is the respondent.

Interdict is broadly equivalent to the English remedy of injunction. The use of the term "injunction" is inappropriate in Scotland. Beware of loose usage by newsreaders and suchlike. When an injunction is awarded by the English courts, for example, against publication or distribution of memoirs in breach of the Official Secrets Act, it has proved necessary to seek separately an interdict in the Court of Session so that the Scottish media also is restrained from publication.

Interdict has no real application in negligence. Interdict is an appropriate remedy in delicts of intention, for example, in defamation, trespass, nuisance and use of land *in aemulationem vicini*. Interdict is used to protect intellectual property rights and is generally applicable in the economic delicts such as passing off or wrongful interference with contracts.

Interdicts must be framed in clear and precise terms so that the party interdicted should be left in no doubt regarding the forbidden activity. The terms of the interdict must be no wider than necessary to curb the wrong complained of.

Interdicts may be permanent — that is, made without limit of time — or interim. An interim interdict is an immediate remedy that may be applied for at any stage in the process of application for a permanent interdict. For example, if an interdict is sought to prevent publication of defamatory material in a newspaper, an interim interdict may be required if intended publication is imminent. The award of a permanent interdict requires more time and justification, and will not help the petitioner if the material is published before the court reaches a conclusion. The interim interdict serves the purpose of preventing publication, while the more detailed consideration required for permanent interdict takes place.

Interim interdicts are awarded at the court's discretion. There must be a prima facie case; in other words, on the basis of the petitioner's pleadings, it must appear that a relevant case in defamation, or nuisance or whatever wrong is complained of has been made out. The court will then consider the balance of convenience between the parties. For example, it may be argued that the award of interdict will cause a greater wrong to the respondent than the wrong complained of by the petitioner. Any public interest in the activity complained of will be taken into account by the court. Only where the balance of convenience is held to be in the petitioner's favour will interim interdict be granted. An interim interdict is valid until recalled by the court.

In general interdict is only awarded where there is a genuine prospect of future wrongs. Interdict is not competent in respect of an activity that is unlikely to be repeated.

DAMAGES

The purpose of damages is to repair the loss suffered by the pursuer. Damages in Scots law are not intended to penalise and do not reflect the degree of culpability of the delinquent party. In awarding damages the courts seek, insofar as is possible, to effect *restitutio in integrum*, that is to restore pursuers to the position they would have been in had the delict not occurred.

Broadly, claims for damages fall under two heads, solatium and patrimonial loss. Solatium is awarded in respect of pain and suffering, impairment or disfigurement and shortened life expectancy consequent upon personal injury. Solatium is also awarded in respect of affront, for example, in defamation. It may be helpful to distinguish the two forms of solatium. The expression "patrimonial" derives from the Roman concept of *patrimonium*, meaning a person's estate. Patrimonial loss covers all tangible economic losses, including property damage and financial harm.

Where the harm sustained is property damage the process of assessing the quantum (amount) of damages is relatively straightforward. The pursuer may recover from the defender the cost of repairing or replacing the property. Reasonable expenses are also recoverable, so if a car is damaged through negligence the defender may be held liable to pay the costs of a hire car while the original vehicle is being fixed.

Damages in personal injury cases
Where the pursuer has suffered personal injury, the claim for damages in respect of pain and suffering will be under the head of solatium and any derivative financial costs, such as medical expenses and loss of earnings, will be claimed under the head of patrimonial loss.

Placing a monetary value on pain and suffering is an inexact science. The severity and nature of the injuries will be taken into account along with the extent of any disability or loss of amenity. Awareness of pain is relevant, so if the pursuer is in a coma there may be no award of solatium. In practice, close regard is paid to the sums awarded in previous decisions and lawyers make great use of McEwan and Paton's looseleaf guide, *Damages for Personal Injuries in Scotland*. By using this guide it is possible to find out recent awards made in respect of particular injuries. For example, if a client has lost a leg the guide will give details of sums awarded in previous instances of the same injury.

Solatium may be awarded, not only in respect of pain and suffering from the date of injury to the date of proof, but also in respect of future pain and suffering where this is relevant. Where the victim dies, the claim for solatium transmits to the executor. Members of the victim's immediate family have a claim in their own right for what may conveniently termed "loss of society", although strictly speaking this is now the "relative's non-patrimonial award", the common law claim having been replaced by a claim under s.1 of the Damages (Scotland) Act 1976 as amended by the Damages (Scotland) Act 1993. The right to this claim is lost where liability has been excluded or discharged prior to the death of the victim, except where the cause of death is mesothelioma. Mesothelioma is caused by exposure to asbestos. The exception to the general rule in respect of this disease has been introduced by the Rights of Relatives to Damages (Mesothelioma) (Scotland) Act 2007, which seeks to overcome the following problem. Given the very short time between diagnosis and death, around 14 months, the general rule posed pursuers and their families an unfortunate dilemma. Should victims sue for compensation when it was most needed, that is while still alive, or should the claim be postponed until after death when the sum sued for would be much larger because it would include relatives' claims for loss of society? It is now possible to raise the claim during the life of the pursuer without the risk of losing the relatives' claims on death. The elements of the "loss of society" award are: distress endured at witnessing the suffering of the victim; grief and sorrow on death; and loss of the non-patrimonial benefit in terms of society and guidance that would have been derived from the victim had he or she lived

Damages in respect of patrimonial loss cover loss of earnings, outlays and reasonable expenses. A sum may be awarded in respect of necessary services rendered by relatives under s.8 of the Administration of Justice Act 1982. Section 9 of the same Act provides that a sum may be awarded to the victim in respect of services that the victim is no longer able, on account of their injuries, to render the family. This would include such things as vehicle maintenance, childcare and housework. The victim must account to the relatives concerned for any such sums awarded. Where the victim has died, relatives may also recover damages in respect of loss of support and funeral expenses.

Patrimonial loss is subdivided under two further heads, past and future, of which future loss is both the most important and most difficult to calculate. The pursuer may claim for loss of earnings up until the date of proof. The sum payable is net wages or salary. To calculate future earnings the net wage at the date of proof is taken as the multiplicand. The court must determine the number of years over which damages are due in respect of future earnings. This is the multiplier. The multiplier is never as great as the number of years the pursuer has left until retirement, because the pursuer will gain interest on the lump sum awarded and also because nobody can ever be certain they will survive until retirement. The product of the multiplicand and multiplier is then calculated to give a lump sum that can then be invested. Expenses, such as the cost of nursing care, can be taken into account under future losses. Awards of damages, both past and future, will include sums claimed as interest.

Deductions

Damages in respect of patrimonial loss are subject to deductions, firstly in the form of income tax. Earnings or remuneration from an employer, unemployment benefits prior to the date of the award of damages and any benevolent payment received by the pursuer will all be taken into account in reducing the award of damages.

Under the Social Security (Recovery of Benefits) Act 1997 various social security benefits paid to the defender during the "relevant period" must be deducted from the sum payable to the pursuer by the person against whom the award has been made, the compensator. The "relevant period" is five years from the date of the accident or five years from first claiming benefit in respect of "a disease". Where damages are paid within five years of the accident, the relevant period ends at the date of payment. The sum deducted by the compensator from the victim's compensation is then paid directly to the Secretary of State.

Provisional damages

Where it is proved or admitted that there is a risk that the pursuer's health or condition will seriously deteriorate in the future, s.12 of the Administration of Justice Act 1982 provides that a provisional award of damages may be made. Such an award is only permissible where the defender is a public authority or is insured. A provisional award of damages means that the pursuer may seek further damages in future if the risk of serious deterioration materialises. At that stage it will be possible to assess the extent of pain and suffering or any reasonable expenses. It is within the discretion of the court to set a time limit against future claims. Following the decision of the House of Lords in *Rothwell v Chemical and Insulation Co Ltd* the Scottish Parliament has enacted the Damages (Asbestos-Related Conditions) (Scotland) Act 2009. In *Rothwell* pleural plaques were held not to be material harm though they are an indicator that there has been exposure to asbestos and so there is a possibility of asbestos related illness arising in the future. The Scottish courts have made awards of provisional damages in the past where pleural plaques have been identified and the new legislation is intended to allow this to continue. The legality of the new Act is however being challenged in the courts.

Interim damages

The court may grant an award of interim damages before the process of litigation is concluded. Interim payments will only be awarded where liability is admitted by the defender or where there appears no question that the pursuer will succeed. This also means that there should no prospect of a substantial reduction of damages on grounds of contributory negligence.

APPENDIX: SAMPLE EXAMINATION QUESTIONS AND ANSWER PLANS

Appendix: Sample Questions

Q1. Bill is the manager of a foundry. He hears cries and a commotion coming from a part of the foundry 100m away. When he goes to investigate he discovers that there has been a spillage of molten metal and sees two men wrapping a third in a fire blanket. He can see that the victim's clothes are burning. He does not recognise the victim since his face is badly burnt and his hair has gone. He is screaming. At that point a crucible fractures and Bill and the two helpers spring away. The eruption of molten metal engulfs the original victim who burns to death. It dawns on Bill that the victim is his brother-in-law. As a result of the incident Bill suffers clinical depression and insomnia. When he does sleep nightmares awaken him.

The foundry owners admit that the incident occurred as a result of their negligence, but they deny that they owed Bill a duty of care in respect of psychiatric harm. Can Bill recover damages?

Notes for answer

Clearly Bill has suffered loss in the form of a recognised psychiatric illness, so the requirements of *Simpson v ICI* are satisfied. The real issue here is whether Bill should sue as a primary or a secondary victim. Since both appear possible from the text, you should consider both possibilities and evaluate Bill's chances of recovering damages in each.

Bill's best chances of recovering damages are if he can establish himself as a primary victim to whom a duty of care to guard against personal injury was owed. Applying *Page v Smith* he can do this if he can show that he was within the area of potential harm. The facts are very similar to *Campbell v North Lanarkshire County Council* so he should at least be allowed to lead evidence to show that he was in danger. As a back-up argument the case of *Salter v UB Frozen and Chilled Foods Ltd* in which the purser was regarded as a primary victim due to his involvement in the accident may be cited.

If Bill fails to have himself regarded as a primary victim then he must claim as a secondary victim. To recover damages he must satisfy the rules laid down in *Alcock v Chief Constable of South Yorkshire*. Clearly Bill was present during the second incident and witnessed the immediate aftermath of the first with his own senses. Bill must prove close ties of love and affection with his brother-in-law and he will have to lead evidence to prove this. *Alcock* shows that such ties will not be presumed in this type of relationship. You do not know whether Bill will be able to prove this or not, but you might conclude that the requirement of a close tie of love and affection presents a barrier to recovery as a secondary victim that does not apply to Bill's case as a primary victim.

If Bill is to succeed as a primary victim he will have to prove that he was in danger himself, though he may possibly persuade the court to treat him as a primary victim on the basis of his involvement in the events. If he is to succeed as a secondary victim he will have to prove close ties of love and affection with his brother in law.

Q2. The local primary school has a flat roof. The school building is surrounded by an eight foot high wall, although there are places where it is possible for a child aged nine or over to climb to gain access to the school yard. Children have been known to gain access to the school grounds during the summer holidays and have been seen on occasions to play on the roof. They are usually warned off by an adult. No child has ever suffered an accident on the roof.

On this occasion, during the school holidays, three boys aged 14 climb over the wall and gain access to the roof via a rhone pipe. They play tig during which they bounce off plastic skylights. One boy jumps onto a skylight from a height of five feet and crashes through it, falling to his death in the school hall below. It is established in evidence that the school could have installed stronger skylights and boxed in the rones at reasonable expense.

Notes for answer
The facts in this problem are more or less identical to those in *Devlin v Strathclyde Regional Council*. That case should be followed. A duty is owed under s.2(1) of the Occupiers' Liability (Scotland) Act to the boys, even though they are trespassers. Their presence on the roof was foreseeable and the school could have taken further steps to prevent this. Nevertheless, the school cannot be held liable. The standard is that of reasonable care and the school are not required to take every preventative measure possible. At their age, the boys may be deemed to have consented to the risk of injury (see s.2(3)). They had to overcome obvious hurdles to gain access to the roof and they were sufficiently old to have knowledge of the risks. The act of bouncing onto a skylight was particularly reckless and not an event that the school ought to have foreseen or guarded against.

Q3. Kevin works for Murray. Murray lets Kevin take the works van home on instruction that he is to go straight home. Kevin makes a minor detour to pick up some groceries. As he leaves the shop he pulls out into the road, spinning his wheels and without first checking his mirrors. Holly is driving down the road well within the speed limit and paying proper attention. Because Kevin's manoeuvre is so sudden, Holly has to swerve onto the wrong side of the road to avoid a collision. Holly's car stalls and she is unable to start it before Sue ploughs into it on her motorbike. Sue was riding too fast and not paying proper attention.

Sue suffers compound fractures of both legs and her motorbike is damaged beyond repair. Sue's solicitor writes to Murray seeking compensation for her injuries and damage to the bike and threatening legal action. Murray claims that none of this has anything to do with him. Explain the legal position to Murray ignoring the criminal law.

Notes for answer

It is most likely that Murray will be vicariously liable to Sue on the basis that it was Kevin's delictual action that caused her injuries. On the neighbourhood principle in *Donoghue* Kevin owed a duty of care to other road users and pedestrians in the vicinity to guard against accidents. The strong inference from the text is that in pulling onto the road in the way he did Kevin exercised less care than would have been taken by the reasonably careful driver. He has, accordingly, breached his duty. Kevin's bad driving is the *causa sine qua non* of the injuries to Sue. It is also the *causa causans*. Holly's act in swerving across the road was the natural and probable consequence of Kevin's pulling onto the road without care so it is not a *novus actus interveniens* breaking the chain of causation. Reference may be made here to Lord Wright's dictum in *The Oropesa* or to other relevant case law. As Kevin's employer, Murray will be called to answer for the injuries caused by Kevin if vicarious liability can be established. Whether the sufficient connection test from *Lister v Hesley Hall* or the scope of employment test from *Kirby v NCB* is employed, case law is strongly suggestive of vicarious liability. The case most obviously in point here is *McLeod v SSEB* and if that is applied then Murray will be found vicariously liable.

Murray may be advised that liability is joint and several. Sue may choose to pursue an action against him rather than Kevin though she may name both as defenders. In the event that Murray pays compensation to Sue he may in principle recover this from Kevin as demonstrated in *Lister v Romford Ice*. Whether this is a realistic prospect will depend on whether Kevin has any money. Sue will seek damages in solatium for pain and suffering and she will also seek patrimonial damages for the repair or replacement of her bike. The good news for Murray is that any sum awarded Sue in damages is likely to be reduced for contributory negligence under the Law Reform (Contributory Negligence) Act 1945 s.1. The extent to which damages are reduced will reflect the degree to which the court regards Sue as blameworthy for the accident. There could be a substantial reduction here given the facts as stated.

Q4. Harry burns rubbish in his back garden every week at irregular times. The prevailing wind blows the smoke into Jessica's house whenever she opens her windows to air her rooms. Jessica claims that the washing hung out on her clothes line often smells of smoke and her white sheets are spoiled by sooty deposits. She has often complained to Harry.

Advise Jessica on any remedy she may seek. How would you advise her if a valuable damask table cloth has been ruined?

Notes for answer

Jessica may seek to interdict Harry from burning rubbish in his garden or, given that interdicts must be framed no more widely than necessary to obviate the harm complained of she may seek to interdict him from burning rubbish in such a way as to cause nuisance. An interdict could be framed in terms that restricted Harry's burning to certain times or perhaps when the wind was not blowing towards Jessica's property. Jessica is more likely to succeed with this than an attempt to stop the burning outright.

To obtain any remedy Jessica must establish nuisance. She must establish that the harm or inconvenience complained of is *plus quam tolerabile* (more than reasonably tolerable) in the circumstances. *Watt v Jamieson*, 1954 S.C. 56 must be cited as laying down this requirement. The court has to balance Harry's right to do on his land anything that is lawful against Jessica's right to the comfortable enjoyment of her property. Disturbance must be serious, inconvenience substantial, in other words Jessica must show that the harm is material and given the facts this ought to be the likely outcome.

Jessica may be advised to seek damages in respect of the damask table cloth. It is important to note that, in addition to establishing nuisance, she requires to establish *culpa* where damages are sought on the authority of *RHM Bakeries Ltd v Strathclyde Regional Council*, 1985 S.L.T. 214. Fault in nuisance may be relevantly pled in terms of a deliberate act done in the knowledge that harm will be the likely result (*Kennedy v Glenbelle*, 1996 S.C. 95). Knowledge of harm may be constructive (*Anderson v White*, 2000 S.C. 392), but in this case Harry has been specifically informed of the damage his activities are causing so he has that knowledge and his persistence is culpable. Since *culpa* can be established Jessica should have her damages.

INDEX